SCTA
Racing News
10¢ A COPY

PROGRAM

Sept. 28th 1941

Wally Parks
Merl Finkenbinder

GrapkE LESLIE LONG

MUROC LAKE TIME TRIALS
So. Calif. Timing Association

25-26, 1948 25¢

g Association, Inc

COUNCIL DRIVE

Sou

S. C. T. A.

IN TH

S. C. T. A.
Racing News
OGRA

THE BIRTH OF HOT RODDING

THE STORY OF THE DRY LAKES ERA

ROBERT GENAT AND DON COX   FOREWORD BY WALLY PARKS

MOTORBOOKS
INTERNATIONAL

This edition first published in 2003 by Motorbooks International, an imprint of MBI Publishing Company, Galtier Plaza, Suite 200, 380 Jackson Street, St. Paul, MN 55101-3885 USA.

The information in this book is true and complete to the best of our knowledge. All recommendations are made without any guarantee on the part of the author or Publisher, who also disclaim any liability incurred in connection with the use of this data or specific details.

We recognize that some words, model names and designations, for example, mentioned herein are the property of the trademark holder. We use them for identification purposes only. This is not an official publication.

Motorbooks International titles are also available at discounts in bulk quantity for industrial or sales-promotional use. For details write to the Special Sales Manager at Motorbooks International Wholesalers & Distributors, Galtier Plaza, Suite 200, 380 Jackson Street, St. Paul, MN 55101-3885 USA.

Library of Congress Cataloging-in-Publication Data

Genat, Robert, 1945-
   The birth of hot rodding / by Robert Genat.
      p. cm.
   Includes bibliographical references.
   ISBN 0-7603-1303-2 (hard : alk. paper)
    1. Automobile racing—California—Mojave Desert—History.
    2. Hot Rods—California—Mojave Desert—History. I. Title.

GV1033 .G46 2003
792.72'09794'95—dc21

On the front cover: Phil Remington, a member of the *Low Flyers* club, confers with his friends before he runs his 239-ci Mercury-powered Streamliner down the course at El Mirage. This car ran consistently at 130 miles per hour.

On the end papers: A full program that listed each entrant's name and equipment was printed for every sanctioned SCTA and Russetta meet. Many of the SCTA programs featured the beautiful artwork of Gus Maanum. His drawings captured the speed and romance of competition on the lakes.

On the frontispiece: The timing tag was the ultimate badge of honor given to those who raced on the dry lakes. This brass tag was undeniable proof that the car was indeed as fast as claimed. The speed for Don Cox's street-driven B roadster was nowhere near the class record, but it proved he was a participant. Many competitors attached these tags to the instrument panels of their cars.

On the title page: It's July 18, 1948, at El Mirage dry lake. The sun has just come up and the chill of the desert night has yet to burn off. To fight the early morning cold, spectators and drivers wear warm clothes. Three lanes of roadsters are ready to run the dusty course. Tension is in the air as each driver hopes to push his roadster to a higher speed.

On the foreword page: Wally Parks' contribution to American motorsports is legendary. He was one of the original organizers of the SCTA, its first postwar president, and subsequently its general manager. Parks also drove the Burke-Francisco belly tank car from 1947 through 1949, and he was the first editor of *Hot Rod* magazine. Through Parks' efforts, the SCTA was allowed to race at Bonneville. In 1951, he formed and was the first president of the National Hot Rod Association (NHRA)— the world's largest motorsports sanctioning body. Parks didn't invent land speed racing or drag racing, but he helped organize both into safe and structured events. In the process, Parks single-handedly made hot rodding respectable. Here, a youthful Wally Parks, dressed in a sport coat, slacks, and stylish argyle socks, sits on the running board of the SCTA's truck. *Greg Sharp Collection*

On the back cover, top right: Emil Dietrich's Streamliner had a fully chromed front end. Many Streamliners, like Dietrich's, were converted Modifieds. On April 24, 1948, this car ran down the dusty El Mirage dry lake at a speed of 144.46 miles per hour. **Top left:** James Bradford of the *Whistlers Club* sits in his roadster and waits for his turn to race across the hard-packed surface of El Mirage Dry Lake at full speed. Bradford's car is a typical street roadster that raced on the dry lakes. He mounted a 1929 Ford Model A roadster body on a 1932 Ford frame and added a 1941 Mercury V-8 engine. This combination was known as an "A V-8." Bradford also added a 1932 grille shell with a set of custom bars. Bradford had to remove the headlights and windshield, add a tarp over the passenger compartment, and use leather straps to secure the hood in order to race. **Bottom:** Barney Navarro was an intense man who was an expert machinist and understood the magic of an internal combustion engine. He was an early pioneer in Flathead speed equipment and supercharging. Navarro was able to squeeze more horsepower from fewer cubic inches than anyone else. This roadster, powered by a small 182-ci Flathead, ran over 119 miles per hour at the lakes.

Printed in Hong Kong

CONTENTS

FOREWORD
My First Trip to the Dry Lakes
By Wally Parks

I vividly remember my first trip to the dry lakes. After all the anticipation and last-minute preparations, a late night's journey to Muroc dry lake and arrival at that legendary expanse of desert vastness was a one-time experience, never to be matched or ever forgotten. The nearest thing to it, as I thought then, would be like landing on the moon!

That was in 1932, when three of us young guys headed north out of Los Angeles in a 1925 Model T Ford coupe with its freshly installed 1929 Model A Flathead engine. We breezed up the highway and into the mountains, relishing the power and ease with which our conveyance mastered the steep grades and turns of old Mint Canyon Road. Then up near the summit, we suddenly lost our forward momentum. The engine was running fine, but the rest of the vehicle rolled to a standstill.

As we sat there looking helpless at the side of a road with no sign of oncoming traffic, a big flatbed truck and trailer came around the bend. Its driver stopped to ask if we were having problems. The outcome was that he towed us uphill to a closed roadside café, where we parked the T and he offered us a lift up to Lancaster, his journey's end of the line. We all rode on the back of the open flatbed under a star-filled sky, drinking in the warm summer night's air.

At about three in the morning, we were stranded in front of a little store/café that stayed open to accommodate a trickle of dry lakes adventurers before they turned off the highway and into the desert. As we stood outside, two young men of about our age came out to their car, and we asked if we might hitch a ride to the lakebed.

Their obliging answer was "yes—if you can fit in!" It was a tight squeeze, but we managed to fit three

guys in the rumble seat of a full-fendered, top-up, 1931 Ford roadster and were very thankful for the rescue.

We sped through the night until turning off from the highway above Lancaster, where we headed east, cross-country on a rutted trail through sand and sagebrush. Overhead was one of the brightest moons one could ever have imagined and the fresh desert air was euphoric. After zigzagging for miles in this unbelievable approach, we rode past the old store and postoffice and, shortly before daylight, we emerged on the near-white, moonlit edge of that dried expanse of flat desert surface called Muroc (now Rogers) dry lake.

Here and there were cars sprinkled along the lakebed's edge—their occupants grabbing a few winks or huddled around campfires, awaiting the coming of sunrise and action. A few eager beavers were already out there, making predawn test runs despite the dangerous risks.

As the sun finally peeked over mountains far to the east, there was a stirring of cars and people emerging from overnight locations and heading for the racecourse and assembly area. For us, the fresh new morning and its promising "first experience" were a bonus, well worth the inconvenience of being on foot and not having a clue as to how we might be getting ourselves back home.

After hanging around the starting line, looking at the cars, and watching the meet get started, we decided to walk the spectator side of the course to the finish line and timing traps, some 2 miles away. It was a longer hike than we had envisioned, but cars racing through the course and an audience of trackside onlookers added new dimensions of excitement to the whole spectacle. Feeling hot, tired, thirsty, and having

no available shade made little difference to us. We were in our own special mecca, with never-to-be-forgotten sights and sounds being firmly implanted as memories of that very special day.

That I volunteered to man a mid-course "observation post"—sitting on a wooden crate in the back of an old dump truck with a military field phone headset clamped to my ear—was an experience that topped it all. I was on a party line circuit that linked start- and finish-area officials, tuned in to the full details of an auto racing event's operations! I even had a chance to alert them of two racecars approaching one another in opposite directions during the two-way record runs, but which passed each other harmlessly.

It was that first day's experience and the awareness of details of responsibility that may have triggered my later interest in the planning and administration of automotive performance activities and, in following

years, a lifetime of exciting, unusual, and often rewarding involvement.

Oh, yes—about that stranded Model T coupe in Mint Canyon? After we caught rides with friends after leaving the lakes meet, it was still there, patiently waiting, with sheared ring-gear rivets in its Model T differential and ready for the long tow back home.

Of all such events that followed, none matched the feeling of magic that was part of that first visit to the dry lakes, where man, machine, and Mother Nature combined their unique and individual features into an overall spirit of challenge and achievement.

It began as a source of shared personal enjoyment— sans prizes or purse money—and that wholesome tradition remains solid today. In terms of sheer personal satisfaction, little can equal the lure of running hot rods at the dry lakes.

DEDICATION

To David Newhardt—a wonderful friend and world-class photographer.

ACKNOWLEDGMENTS

First and foremost, I must thank my friend Don Cox for his excellent dry lakes photos. He was only 10 years old when he got his first camera. Prior to World War II, Don worked in several photo labs and camera stores. He joined the Navy on December 8, 1941—the day after the attack on Pearl Harbor. The Navy was smart enough to make him a Photographer's Mate. While he was in the Navy, Don was exposed to rounds from Japanese guns, as well as many types of film and cameras. He honed his skills, and after the war, he continued to take photos. When Don went to the lakes in the 1940s to race his Roadster with the *Oilers* club, he took his cameras. He also took along the then-new 35mm Kodachrome slide film. Kodachrome was designed to be fine-grained and archival. All of Don's color images in this volume were shot on that film. He also shot black-and-white images on several different types of film in various formats. Don captured the cars and the feeling of a lakes event. After shooting the photos myself for over 20 of my books, I never thought I'd work on a project with anyone else's images—but this is the one. Thanks Don!

As a kid, I used to read *Hot Rod* magazine. I never thought I'd ever see then-editor Wally Parks in person, much less meet him. Now, I'm proud to say we are friends. I wrote Wally with a little hesitation to ask if he'd write the foreword for this book. He quickly and graciously agreed. Wally's recollection of his first trip to the lakes sets the perfect tone for this book. I'm deeply honored by the fact that he consented to be a part of my book. I must also thank him for answering my many questions. Not many people get to know honest-to-goodness legends on a first-name basis, but I have. His friendship has enriched my life. Thanks Wally!

Many thanks must also go out to the men who pioneered lakes racing and allowed me to interview them for this book. Thanks to dry lakes heroes Stu Hilborn, Fred Lobello, Alex Xydias, Jim Nelson, Jack Calori, and Bill Burke. Thanks also to Chuck Edwald of the *San Diego Roadster* club, Greg Sharp of the NHRA Motorsports Museum, Clara Jo Ostergren of the *San Fernando Model T* club, David Bloomberg of the *Sidewinders*, and Jim "J.D." Tone of the *San Diego Roadster* club. A big thanks must go to Jack Underwood for maintaining the SCTA archives and sharing them with me. Thanks to Dain Gingerelli for sharing his dry lakes research materials and editorial advice. Thanks must also go to Lee Klancher, senior editor and friend at Motorbooks. When I sent Lee two sheets of Don Cox's slides, he saw right away how special these photos were and he had the same vision as I did of what this book should be.

INTRODUCTION

The Mojave Desert was a most unlikely place for the birth of hot rodding. Located approximately 100 miles northeast of Los Angeles, one has to cross over the San Gabriel Mountains to get there. In the Mojave Desert, temperatures can range from below freezing to as high as 134 degrees Fahrenheit. The landscape extends from 282 feet below sea level to 11,049 feet above. The Mojave Desert is a foreboding place that confirms that either God made a mistake or he has a cruel sense of humor. It's the kind of place where people go when they no longer want to be found. The Mojave is also a place where atom bombs were tested, the first sonic booms were heard, and where early Roadsters ripped across a dry lakebed at full throttle.

A desert is defined as an area that annually receives less than 10 inches of rain, with a rate of evaporation that exceeds that of the rain it receives. The Mojave receives an average of 1 to 5 inches of rain per year with a potential evaporation rate of 70 inches. What little rain falls on the Mojave comes in the form of winter storms. Unfortunately, the surrounding mountains absorb the moisture from these storms, leaving little for the lower elevations.

The Mojave is characterized by brown-colored mountains covered with sand, rocks, and spiny Joshua trees. The rain from the mountains runs down into *bajadas*, long sedimentary slopes that descend gently to the desert floor. Within these bajadas grow a few cactus and the aromatic creosote bush. The bajadas pour into large basins which have no outlet. The desert heat quickly evaporates the water from these basins, leaving behind an alkaline silt. After thousands of cycles of rain, runoff, and evaporation, a dry lake is formed. At one time, all of the dry lakes in the Mojave contained water year-round; but changing geological and weather patterns transformed these areas into dry lakes. The only time they contain water today is after an infrequent rainfall or snowfall. The occasional rain floods the dry lakebeds and smoothes out any irregularities, leaving a crust as flat as a billiard table.

Dry lakes are scattered throughout the Mojave. The ones closest to Los Angeles are Rosamond, Muroc (which today is called Rogers) and El Mirage. Harper, Cuddeback, Goldstone, and Bicycle dry lakes were also used for racing. These lakes, and a few others, were smaller in size and a much farther drive from Los Angeles. They also didn't have the excellent surface of Muroc. At 44 square miles, Muroc is the largest of the dry lakes and the favorite of the early racers. In the late 1800s it was called Rodriguez Dry Lake, but was eventually anglicized into "Rodgers." The name was ultimately shortened to "Rogers."

In 1910, the Corum family, who had immigrated from Scotland, settled at the edge of Rogers dry lake bed. They raised alfalfa and turkeys and helped settle new homesteaders into the area for a fee of $1 per acre. As others moved in, the Corums drilled wells and cleared land for the new residents. In addition, they also opened a general store and post office. They wanted to have the post office stop named "Corum," after themselves, but it was disallowed because there was already a "Coram," California. So they reversed the spelling of their name and came up with "Muroc." Soon, the dry lake became known as Muroc. When the Army Air Corps moved in, the base was named Muroc. In 1942, Muroc dry lake reverted to being called Rogers under the control of the Army Air Corps.

Rosamond dry lake is located southwest of Muroc. It is half the size of Muroc, but is exceptionally flat. Across a 5.5 mile span of the lakebed, there is only an 18-inch crown. Portions of these lakes, as well as the smaller Buckhorn that lies in between, were used by the Army Air Corps in the 1930s for bombing and gunnery practice. During World War II, a 650-foot wooden replica of a Japanese warship was constructed on Rogers dry lake for aerial practice. This ship, sitting in the middle of an apparent ocean of shimmering heat waves, surprised many people driving on the road that parallels the lake. It was on Muroc dry lake that the first organized time trials were held in the 1920s.

The Muroc Racing Association (MRA) held its first meet on May 8, 1932. These early MRA meets were loosely organized with as many as five cars running across the lakebed at one time. Only the driver of the front-running car had a clear view ahead. Those trailing behind were lost in the billowing clouds of dust that the leaders created. Those in the back, blinded by rooster tails of dust, often ran into each other or into an obstruction on the lake's surface that they were unable to see. The frail cars would flip and tumble, sending parts and drivers flying. Those lucky enough to survive a high-speed wreck were administered first aid by fellow racers. A trip to the emergency room was often as painful as the wreck, because the nearest hospital was 30 miles away and not all the roads that led to the hospital were paved. The early days on the lakes were for the hearty and foolhardy.

With the formation of the Southern California Timing Association (SCTA) in 1937, structure and safety were added to the events. In addition to the SCTA, the other major dry lakes sanctioning body was the Russetta Timing Association (RTA). The primary difference between the two associations was the fact that Russetta had a class for coupes and sedans, whereas the SCTA was limited to roadsters. Both organizations were made up of local clubs. There were very few clubs that belonged to both sanctioning bodies.

World War II had a dramatic effect on dry lakes racing. Both Rosamond and Muroc were permanently claimed by the Army Air Corps. Many of the men who raced on the lakes joined one of the branches of the military. There they utilized their Flathead tuning skills on the Allison engines of the P-51 Mustangs. Many traded their wrenches for a rifle and parked their hot rod for a Jeep. A large contingent stayed in the Los Angeles area working for North American Aviation building P-51s, or working for Lockheed in Burbank building P-38s. Hot rodding would continue on a very low-key basis. Gasoline and tires had been rationed, making a lengthy trip to the dry lakes a foolish waste of precious raw materials. Between July 1942, and April 1946, there were no organized dry lakes meets. In their spare time, stateside soldiers tinkered with their cars and those overseas made plans for their return to the streets of America and to the dry lakes.

Following the war, racing on the lakes picked up where it left off. The cars that returned after the war were the same ones that ran there prior to the war. They hatched from the cocoon of the family garage and returned to the lakes equipped just as they had been five years earlier. For the duration of the war, the American automotive industry had sat dormant. The effort and might of those industries had been funneled into making war goods. It would be several years before the technology that had been developed during the war would make its way into the automobile. Also dormant during those war years was the hot rod aftermarket industry. Parts had not been produced, but new manufacturing techniques would eventually result in new speed equipment.

Those returning from the war were anxious to pick up where they had left off. They were also anxious to enjoy life. The government helped by providing each veteran with a generous separation bonus and the GI Bill, which extended education benefits and low-cost loans for housing. Those returning to the lakes from the battles in Europe and the Pacific were more mature in their approach to speed and to life in general. While away, they had plenty of time to think about how to make their cars go faster.

Also following the war, West Coast aircraft companies shifted from building propeller-driven fighters to building sleek new jets. Visionaries saw that there would be a boom in commercial air travel and began a plan of modifying World War II military transports into plush airliners. All of this led to plenty of work in the Southern California area and lots of available surplus aircraft parts to adapt to hot rods.

The first meet following the war was held at El Mirage dry lake on April 4, 1946. It was sponsored by the SCTA. Both Rosamond and Muroc dry lakes would continue to be controlled by Edwards Air Force Base and no meets were held on those lakes. El Mirage became the new mecca for dry lakes racing and attendance at the races continually grew. Thousands of people would turn out to see the cars run. New clubs were being formed so members could run their newly built hot rods on the lakes. New speed equipment was continually being developed for the venerable Ford Flathead. The old equipment was being sold to those new to hot rodding, in a tradition of recycling that continues today. The SCTA revised its rules to make racing safer and worked the public relations side to convince the general public that hot rodders were not a threat to society.

Many of the early lakes racers developed equipment for their personal car that would allow it to go faster. Vic Edelbrock developed intake manifolds and cylinder heads and ran a 1932 roadster. Today Edelbrock is a multimillion-dollar company that provides all types of performance parts to automotive enthusiasts. Stu Hilborn, the first lakes racer to run 150 miles per hour on the lakes with his Streamlinertreamliner, developed his fuel injection system that revolutionized all forms of auto racing. Fred Carrillo, Mickey Thompson, Alex Xydias, Otto Crocker, Ak Miller, Wally Parks, and many others raced on the lakes and made major contributions to racing and to the hot rodding world. They had no idea or intention of becoming famous—they just wanted to race.

West Coast hot rodders wanted to race more than once a month. To get more racing time, hot rodders turned to the streets. Accidents resulted, in which innocent motorists were often hurt or killed. The solution was to bring the excitement of the lakes to the local neighborhoods on a weekly basis at drag strips. Dotting the West Coast landscape after the war were dozens of unused military and emergency airstrips. These fields were built to accommodate the large number of aircraft that were being built and tested in the area and to provide bases for defense of the coastline. The average runway was 1 mile long and wide enough for two cars to race safely. Test runs determined that 1/4 mile would be the perfect length in which to have a race with 3/4 mile to stop safely.

Hot rodders no longer had to make the long trek to the desert's inhospitable dry lakes to race. Racing was within a short drive and the drag strips accepted all types of cars. There were also no requirements of club membership to participate. There was a class for every type of car, even the family sedan. Drag racing also allowed lakes competitors to race head-to-head, instead of against the clock. Terminal velocity was not as fast as on the lakes, but drag racing's wheel-to-wheel competition, frequency of meets, and proximity to home made it an instant favorite of hot rodders. Lakes racers were able to easily convert their Roadsters and coupes for drag strip competition. Many never returned to the lakes. Drag racing flourished and lakes racing nearly became extinct.

There are those whose love for the dry lakes has persisted and this small contingent of hard-core racers has kept the flame alive. SCTA meets are still held at El Mirage and Bonneville. While drag racing has turned commercial, the dry lakes racers are much the same as they were 50 years ago—an unpretentious lot who simply enjoy the thrill of going fast.

DRY LAKES
HISTORY

When lakes racing became popular in the 1920s, the Model T was the preferred car because of its low cost and available speed equipment. Lakes racers favored the Roadster, but touring cars were also raced. This Model T has been updated with a Flathead engine and twin-carburetor intake. Look closely to see the "brody" knob on the steering wheel.

The first time someone took a car or motorcycle at full throttle across a dry lake was never documented. It's hard to imagine how these desolate locations were discovered in the first place. The Mojave Desert is an inhospitable place to take a joy ride on a sunny Sunday afternoon. The cars of the early 1900s lacked the power to easily climb the mountains from Los Angeles to the desert, and they frequently overheated. Whoever found the dry lakes realized a vehicle could run at full throttle for an extended period of time in almost any direction. The feeling of running a car wide open on a dry lake is much like being in the only speedboat on a smooth lake; there are no road markings, no guideposts, and no speed limit. Whoever made the first runs eventually told others, and soon dust clouds were following legions of frail old cars across the dry lakes. What started out as a single high-speed fling was given structure and turned into a motorsports event.

Muroc dry lake was the site of American Automobile Association (AAA) sanctioned speed events in the 1920s. In May 1923, Joe Nikrent set a record of 108.24 miles per hour in a stripped-down Buick. A year later, Tommy Milton ran 151.26 miles per hour in a Miller-powered race car. In 1927, Frank Lockhart ran 171 miles per hour. Lockhart was an early Los Angeles hot rodder who built his first car from junk parts when he was 16 years old. He won the Indianapolis 500 in 1926, and was killed two years later in an attempt to set a high-speed record at Daytona. Lockhart was a hero to many young men who grew up in the Los Angeles area in the 1920s. They wanted to build cars like his and set speed records.

Early lakes racers realized that their cars could run faster if the cars were lighter and devoid of any external component that could cause wind resistance. The cars' looks were probably inspired by Henry Ford's 999 racer driven by Barney Oldfield, or by the early Vanderbilt Cup

Doug Caruthers was a veteran lakes racer and a member of the *Road Runners* club. Over the years of competition, he raced his modified with a series of four-cylinder engines, including a Ford Model T engine with a Rajo conversion, a Winfield-equipped Ford Model A engine, and a Ford Model B engine with a Cragar conversion. As the Flathead V-8s became more popular, he ran various models. When this photo was taken in 1947, the engine was a 1946 Mercury with Navarro heads and an intake built by Johnny Johnson. This car set the B Streamliner record at 136.39 mph.

SCTA rules for its Roadster classes dictated a stock body. This Model T body is stock, but it has a unique grille shell and hood. A modified Flathead engine is under the hood. The engine's cubic-inch displacement determined the roadster's class. A tarp covered the passenger compartment to help the car's aerodynamics. This car was run by Doug Caruthers in 1947.

racers. These cars were stripped-down, open-wheeled Roadsters and were the fastest motorcars of the era.

Early Dry Lakes Races

On October 9, 1927, the Southern California Championship Sweepstakes were held on Muroc dry lake. Earl Mansell of Pasadena, California, organized the event. The entry blank listed five events, and the cost of entry was $3 per event. The first class was for Ford roadsters. It was open to any Ford roadster, and the owner could run with or without fenders or windshield. Entries in the Ford roadster event were required to have a hood and turtle deck (rear body). The second event was for Ford coupes. Cars for this event were required to have fenders, hood, windshield, and doors. Ford touring cars were scheduled for the third event; fenders and windshield were optional. The fourth event was called the Special Flathead Race and was open to any body style and type of car as long as it had a Flathead engine. Any

winner of the three previous events would have their entry fee refunded for the Flathead race. The final race was the Championship Sweepstakes. It was open to any roadster, coupe, or touring car, and the competitors could run without windshield or fenders. There is no documentation of the results or subsequent events promoted by Mansell. There is no doubt that there were other promoters like Mansell who fed the speed-hungry appetites of those who wanted to test the speed of their cars on the dry lakes.

On March 25, 1931, the Gilmore Oil Company sponsored several dry lakes events. This was the first step toward organized dry lakes meets. George Wight, then-owner of Bell Auto Parts, saw the potential of regular meets sponsored by a major company. Bell Auto Parts, in Bell, California, opened in 1923 and specialized in race car parts. In 1931, Wight invited Los Angeles–area dry lakes enthusiasts to the shop to discuss the organization of dry lake events. The first classifications based on engine types came out of that

Charles Clark of the *Clutchers* club ran this Model A roadster in 1948. It ran in the B Roadster class, which required an unmodified body. The body is stock, but Clark has added plenty of modifications to streamline the car including a belly pan, a 1932 grille shell, and a nosepiece made from a small steel barrel. Masking tape and cardboard have been added to reduce the size of the grille's opening. The car's forward seating position was governed by the rear engine configuration. On July 17, 1948, this car ran 122.61 mph at El Mirage Dry Lake.

meeting. Gilmore provided trophies and prestige to the events. Later in 1931, the Muroc Racing Association (MRA) was formed. The MRA brought in standardized timing equipment (from the Muroc Timing Association), developed a schedule of events, and produced a racing program. Gilmore supported the MRA and bought a full-page ad in each program. Many other automotive-related businesses also saw the advertising potential. The top speeds at the events held in 1932 and 1933 were just under 110 miles per hour. A few racers, such as Joe Mozzetti, were able to hit 116 miles per hour. Mozzetti and Frank Lyons, who ran 112 miles per hour, both ran Riley-modified four-cylinder Ford engines in their roadsters. A majority of the hotter cars ran between 80 and 90 miles per hour. This was also the time when multiple cars ran in one single race.

Throughout the mid-1930s, four-cylinder engines remained popular. These engines had been thoroughly developed, there was a wealth of speed equipment available for them, and they were bulletproof. The new Ford

V-8s had potential, but it would be a few years before anyone built speed equipment on the scale of what was available for the four-cylinder engine. For every V-8 in 1937, there were nine or ten four-cylinder cars. Cragar, Winfield, and Riley provided popular modifications for the Ford four-cylinder engines. Chevy fours were modified with Olds heads. A stripped-down roadster with a modified four-cylinder engine was capable of 100 miles per hour.

As speed trials continued throughout the 1930s at Muroc and other Southern California dry lakes, other classes were established according to speed and body styles. The events became more refined as problems that cropped up at each meet were solved. One of the biggest challenges was preventing reckless and erratic driving by spectators on and around the course. Participating club members shared in lake patrol duty. These patrols were established under the supervision of the local county's Peace Officers Association. Rules for the spectators and racers alike were listed in the pro-

News of the speeds reached on the dry lakes traveled east, and each year a few brave souls would venture west in their hot rods and test their cars on the lakes. This hot rodder brought his roadster from Ohio. Although he wasn't a member of an SCTA club, he was able to run his car as a guest.

gram. Enforcement of those rules was swift and absolute. As the attendance at the lakes meets grew, a larger organization had to assume responsibility.

Formation of the SCTA

In the fall of 1937, car club activity was at an all-time high in Southern California. More aftermarket equipment was available and the interest in competing on the dry lakes was growing. Often a single club or several clubs would join together and sponsor a lakes meet. Most of these events were understaffed because the events were so large. The informal competition between the clubs that sponsored the early meets was very evident. This set the stage for a larger organization, made up of several clubs, to organize lakes events and have safer, coordinated, and structured competition between the clubs.

On November 29, 1937, representatives from five Southern California car clubs met at the *Throttlers'* Hollywood clubhouse. At this historic meeting, it was agreed that an organization of several clubs would be of benefit to all club members and dry lakes racing. On February 7, 1938, the Southern California Timing Association (SCTA) held its first meeting. At this first meeting, the SCTA elected officers, drew up bylaws, and wrote contest rules. The entry fee for each of the clubs was $20, and the monthly dues were initially $2. By May 1938, the group had purchased its own timing equipment and was ready to sponsor its first race.

On May 15, 1938, the newly formed SCTA hosted its first meet at Muroc. Unfortunately, high winds prevented any races, and 10,000 unruly spectators added to the SCTA's woes that day. Instead of being discouraged,

Race officials selected the best stretch of terrain for the course on the dry lake. Often the area around the starting line was dotted with small berms (lumps of dirt) throughout the course. The driver of this 1932 roadster is following the line of cones through one of those bermed areas. In the distance, and blowing to the left, a cloud of dust left by the previous competitor is visible.

Although the sun is up, the cool of the desert night has yet to burn off and everyone is still bundled in sweaters and jackets. Doug Hartelt of the *Lancers* club makes a few final adjustments to his Roadster before the race. Hartelt accumulated the most points in 1947 and earned the privilege to display the number 1 on the side of his Model T roadster. In 1948, Hartelt held the SCTA B Roadster record of 129.265 mph.

SCTA members were encouraged by the organization and saw the potential of SCTA sanctioned races within this new group. The SCTA's second meet was on July 3, 1938. It was a success, and Ernie McAfee, in his Winfield-powered modified, set a new record of 124 miles per hour. *Sidewinders* member Richy Richards, in a Dixon rocker arm modified V-8, ran 120 miles per hour one way, and 104 on the return for an average of 112 miles per hour. Karl Orr, in his Cragar-powered modified, ran 125 miles per hour on his initial run, but failed to complete his back-up run. Toy Dufer, in his three-port Chevy, spun a few donuts on the starting line at the July meet. For his lack of consideration and unprofessionalism, he was fined $5 and suspended for 90 days. The only other problems the SCTA encountered at its second meet were the large crowd around the timing truck at the finish line and racers "chiseling" into the line of cars waiting to race. Unfortunately, this would be the last SCTA meet at Muroc. Without a specific reason, the U.S. Army informed the SCTA

that Muroc would no longer be available for racing. Undaunted, the SCTA scheduled its next meet for Harper dry lake on August 29, 1938.

The SCTA grew substantially in its first year. By the end of 1938, the SCTA was publishing its *Racing News* newsletter twice a month. It featured artwork by Eldon Snapp and covered all club news, as well as important association news. One of the things developed the first year was a $250 hospital fund for members injured during the races at the lakes. The SCTA continued to fine-tune its meets and rules structure to provide a better environment for racers.

The War Years

The attack on Pearl Harbor on December 7, 1941, changed the lives of everyone in America. The U.S. military recruit depots were flooded with young men who wanted to join. It was a mobilization of men and machinery on a scale never before seen in the world. The SCTA's last race for the duration of the war was on

Sprint cars raced on the lakes as streamliners, and were also known as tail jobs. They were placed in the Streamliner class because of the custom body and smooth tail section. This is Jack McAfee's C streamliner that, over the years, ran with several different engine combinations. During the war, McAfee was a mechanic for Col. Pappy Boyington's Black Sheep squadron. McAfee later became a famous sports car driver.

July 19, 1942, at Harper Dry Lake. The young men who ran on the lakes soon had something more important to do.

Like many other young men in America, Alex Xydias put his car up on blocks and enlisted. "I enlisted as an airplane mechanic even though I had a deferment," says Xydias. "God, I just had to get in the war! It was so stupid to be working in a defense plant when everybody was in the war, but I wanted to be an airplane mechanic—that was the ultimate job—so I enlisted in the Army Air Corps." Xydias first worked

on the T-6 trainer and the P-40 fighter. He then went to gunnery school for the B-17. "Because I had a background as a mechanic, I was the engineer gunner who fired the upper turret that was right behind the pilots. I'm proud of the fact that I graduated third in my class." About the time of Xydias' graduation, the war in Europe was winding down. "The Germans heard I was coming, so they surrendered," says Xydias with a laugh.

Xydias never fired a shot in anger during the war, but he did learn a lot. "I got more out of it as a person,"

Veda Orr was the only woman to compete on the lakes. She drove this 1932 Ford roadster that was prepared by her husband Karl. With speeds consistently in the 120-mph range, she placed 21st in points during the SCTA's 1947 season. During the war, she mailed SCTA newsletters to servicemen overseas, and kept the dry lakes flame burning for those so far away. After the war, she published the first book on the dry lakes racers, *Veda Orr's Lakes Pictorial*.

he says. "I got to understand and appreciate discipline. It gave me a chance to mature. I was so young when I went in. When I came out, I was only 22 years old, but I knew a lot more and was very mature." While Xydias was in the Air Corps, he decided to start his own speed shop business. Xydias also thinks the military had a big effect on hot rodders. "I think they learned to do things better and more safely, too. Good construction became more important because you couldn't do a terrible job in the service. You couldn't get by—you had to learn to do it right." The end result was safer, quality hot rods. "There was no way to apply working on a tank to civilian life, but the fact that you worked on it and learned a lot is what's important."

Dean Batchelor had a tremendous effect on the design of all future streamliners in the late 1940s, but in 1944, he was a member of an aircrew in a B-17 named

Flak Happy. On his 12th mission over Germany, *Flak Happy* turned into a flak magnet. Batchelor was told that a B-17 could fly on two engines, but he found out it couldn't. The plane's pilot did a masterful job and brought the wounded bomber in for a wheels-up landing in a German field. Batchelor and the rest of the crew survived, but were taken prisoner by German soldiers. As they marched from one POW camp to another, the German guards lost their way. After 80 days and 487 miles, Batchelor and the rest of the crew arrived at American lines.

Following the war, Batchelor became friends with Alex Xydias, bought a 1932 roadster, and set out for the lakes. There he raced with "So-Cal Speed Shop" painted on the cowl of his black highboy. Batchelor and So-Cal Speed Shop owner Alex Xydias later collaborated on a streamliner that was the fastest

A certain amount of patience was required of any dry lakes racer while he waited in line to race. With no barriers between spectators and race cars behind the starting line, it was a busy place. This young man is wearing his Navy pea coat to stay warm. This 1934 Ford roadster was owned by Dave Glotch of the *Road Runners*.

On April 25, 1948, Neil Davis made dry lakes history when he clocked a speed of 148.27 mph in this yellow 1927 Model T with black flames. On its return run, it set the two-way record for C roadsters at 138.975 mph. This broke the record the car had set on October 19, 1947, with Eddie Hulse behind the wheel. This roadster was featured on the cover of the first issue of *Hot Rod* magazine, and it was owned by Regg Schlemmer.

Frank English's 1932 roadster was typical of the hot rods that ran at the lakes. It had a mildly modified Mercury engine that allowed English to run 106.50 mph on El Mirage. This was not a spectacular speed for a C roadster, but anything over 100 mph for a street-driven roadster in 1947 was considered noteworthy. English was a member of the *Southern California Roadster* club.

Otto Crocker

In the 1920s, J. Otto Crocker ran motorcycles on the dry lakes with his friends. At that time, a hand-held stopwatch was used to time the motorcycles. The inaccuracy of the hand-held watches led Crocker to develop an electronic timer. His device used sealed rubber hoses to start and stop the battery-powered electric clock. Crocker later developed a clock that used photoelectric cells to actuate the timers. It was first used to time powerboat races in San Diego where Crocker was a Commodore of the *San Diego Powerboat* club.

In 1939, when the *San Diego Road Ramblers* club wanted its own timing device, it asked Crocker to design and build its clocks. The system he built was accurate to 1/100th of a second. The *Road Ramblers* asked Crocker to bring his equipment to the last two SCTA meets in 1939. Soon after, the SCTA adopted Crocker and his equipment as its official timers. Crocker's clocks timed the first SCTA meet at Bonneville. When the San Diego Timing Association started regular drag racing at the Paradise Mesa drag strip in the early 1950s, Crocker and his accurate clocks timed the cars. The entire racing world owes Otto Crocker a debt of gratitude for his technical achievements.

American hot rod in 1949 and 1950 at Bonneville.

In 1941, Jack Calori was an inspector for the Douglas Aircraft Company, which earned him a deferment from military service. "Every time I went through the tunnel into the plant from across Lakewood Boulevard, there was a poster of Marines and sailors. I thought it would be great to get into the Navy. I told Douglas I was quitting and I was told, 'You can't quit; your job is essential, it's wartime. You have to stay here and work.' "Calori visited a Navy recruiter and he was told the same thing. He put pressure on Douglas and they transferred him to the day shift and gave him a 10-cent-an-hour raise in an attempt to keep him happy and on the job. One of the perks of working the day shift was lunchtime entertainment from the big bands. "It was nice to hear Tommy Dorsey at lunchtime, but I still wanted to join the Navy." Calori again went to the Navy recruiter and this time when asked where he was working replied, "I'm not!" He was soon sworn in, off to boot camp, and training to be an aviation machinist.

Calori was determined to get on an aircraft carrier and signed up for the *Enterprise*. He was sent to Honolulu and attached to the Naval Air Transport Service. "I didn't go anywhere," says Calori. "I finally gave up the idea of being on an aircraft carrier. I stayed there in Honolulu until the end of the war." While Calori was in Honolulu, he met race car driver Kenny Palmer. "Palmer happened to be the number one driver for J.C. Agajanian. He drove the big Offenhauser jobs." Calori also got to know another lakes racer, Jack McAffee of the *Throttlers*. "We were bunk mates. We didn't talk too much about cars until later. After the war, I found out that he was a driver for Ferrari. He drove at Nuremberg and also in Italy." While in the service, McAffee repaired airplanes for the legendary Col. Pappy Boyington, commander of the Black Sheep Squadron.

Calori brought a lot to hot rodding from his Navy training. "I learned to use ball bearings rather than roller bearings for less friction," says Calori. "The rear

One of the goals of the sanctioning bodies was to impose a small degree of organization at events. The SCTA had a hand-drawn map in each program to outline the course. There were also areas designated for competitors and spectators. The unmarked, large open spaces encouraged capricious parking. Here, a gaggle of roadsters was randomly parked, and faced in the general direction of the starting line.

end on my roadster was machined out and ball bearings were installed. Rather than the 140-weight grease, I used a 90-weight gear oil—that helped me on speed." Calori also realized less weight equaled more horsepower. He did everything he could to reduce weight in his roadster, including driving on the street without front brakes. Calori also learned how important the valves were to efficient engine operation. "When you're doing valves, they had to be right on. You couldn't be sloppy."

Veda Orr has been affectionately called hot rodding's "First Lady." In the 1930s, she helped her

husband Karl Orr race his roadster on the lakes. At that time, lakes racing was strictly a man's world; but in 1937, Veda convinced her husband to let her drive the roadster. She was soon hooked and became the first woman to drive the lakes under SCTA sanction. When racing stopped for the duration of World War II, Veda took over the SCTA newsletter responsibilities from Wally Parks and Eldon Snapp. She mailed sailors and soldiers the SCTA newsletters for free while they were overseas. Once the war was over, she returned to help her husband and race on the lakes. Her fastest time was 132 miles per hour. Veda was also the first person to write a book on dry lakes racing. Much of the early history of the dry lakes was recorded in her book, *Veda Orr's Hot Rod Pictorial*. For a short time following the war, Veda and Karl published the *CT News* (*California Timing News*) that covered dry lakes and circle track events.

Orr's wartime newsletters featured a column entitled, "Letters From The Boys." The column featured notes from dry lakes racers worldwide. This column was a gathering place where servicemen could keep tabs on their friends and remain in contact with the sport they loved. Sgt. Wally Parks, a *Road Runners* member stationed in the Philippines, wrote about the Jeep he built from spare parts, complete with a V-8 60

Most of the cars that ran at the lakes used Ford and Chevrolet engines. These engines were readily available, easy to work on, and inexpensive. This lakes competitor has installed an early 1930s Cadillac V-16. These engines were powerful and were equipped with hydraulic lifters, but they were expensive and there was no additional speed equipment available.

The variety of roadsters that ran on the lakes was endless. Here are two very different examples of street-driven hot rods. The Model T in the foreground is much smaller than the 1932 in the background. The Model T's smaller size and lighter weight worked in its favor on the lakes, but made for a cramped car on the street. The 1932 was much more comfortable, and it offered an optional rumble seat.

Bill Burke was the one who brought the belly tank design to the dry lakes after the war, and all of his cars were built with a single tank. Howard Johansen built this unusual car from two 165-gallon tanks with 4-foot sections added to the center of each. The tank on the left was for the driver, and the tank on the right mounted the Flathead engine. The rear wheels were driven through a unique chain-drive system.

engine: "Things are going fine and my little V-Jeep is really a peach. Just got through putting a spray job on it. It really goes, and I claim to have the hottest thing on the island." Lt. Colonel J. F. "Tex" Roberts of the *Throttlers* wrote from Italy about the work of hot rodders (hot jobs): "My job is still engines and airplanes in the inspection line. I'm the air inspector of a wing, and I can truthfully say that the 'hot-job' business has given a number of our boys that knack of ingenuity that is needed to keep machines going when the right part isn't handy, which is the case quite often here in a combat zone." Army Pvt. Akton Miller wrote from a hospital in England: "I was in the Battle of the Bulge in Belgium and I froze my feet, so I landed here in a hospital in England. I have been looking at this foreign equipment and I'm getting some very nice surprises, especially from the Krauts. They certainly have some super equipment. The English certainly are blower crazy with their small engines. They have developed some swell blowers. I'll be glad to get back home and hop in my little Cad, as there's no greater thrill to me than a good, hot acceleration race." Ens. Joe Bruman of the *Lancers* wrote from somewhere in the Pacific: "I'm as far from a hop-up as I'll ever be."

One of the many catch phrases during World War II was "Home Alive in '45." Many of the lakes racers never made it back from overseas. Those who survived returned with a different perspective on life. They had matured beyond their years and were ready to accept new challenges. Many of them pulled their hot rods off the blocks, filled them with gas, and hit the streets. Those who had sold their cars while overseas, or who

Gear Grinders club member Bob Reese brought this 1932 Ford roadster out to El Mirage in 1947. The 1932 roadsters were not the fastest on the lake, but they were everyone's favorite because of their excellent styling and V-8 power. The small exhaust pipe barely visible under the frame is the "lakes pipe" that was designed to be opened at the lakes.

Spectators and competitors alike came out to the lakes the night before an event, and many camped out with their sleeping bags right by the starting line. Everyone was awakened by the sound of open exhausts at morning's first light, and they had a ringside seat for all the upcoming action.

were new to hot rodding, searched for new iron to modify and race.

Postwar Racing

On April 28, 1946, the SCTA resumed the races on the lakes. The initial meet was the first time many of the racers had seen their buddies who had fought in the war. The cars were unchanged from the last meet four years earlier, but the people had matured. Many who were new to the sport also attended. They may have met someone in the service who had raced on the lakes, or they may have been stationed on the West Coast and heard about the high speeds reached on the flat lake surface.

Five meets were held in 1946, and there were six in 1947. Each of the meets was a one-day event. Due to the growing number of participants, the SCTA decided to run two-day meets in 1948. The Russetta Timing Association (RTA or Russetta) was also formed in 1948. Unlike the SCTA, the Russetta had classifications for coupes and sedans. The SCTA and Russetta were amicable rivals in promotion of lakes racing events. Each association was made up of clubs and structured its events in a similar manner. Many competitors belonged to two clubs, one affiliated with the SCTA and one with Russetta. With two affiliations, the competitors could race at the lakes twice as often. Russetta was looked down upon by the SCTA

because it ran closed cars and didn't have Otto Crocker's excellent timers. Eventually, the SCTA relented and allowed coupes to run.

On Tuesday, October 14, 1947, the first sonic boom was heard over the Mojave Desert. It confirmed that the military would always have possession of Muroc. It also meant there was a new generation of speed enthusiasts in America—in the air and on the land. While Capt. Chuck Yeager's accomplishments were kept secret, young men all over Southern California learned about hot rods and dry lakes speed trials. Dry lakes racing grew at a phenomenal rate.

In 1948, Ak Miller was SCTA's president and raced this D roadster to a speed of 120.48 mph. He was also one of the most inventive competitors on the lakes. There was a 1937 Cadillac V-8 engine in the rear of this car. The nose was half of a belly tank grafted onto a 1923 Dodge roadster body. In the background is Hal's Short Stop Snaks stand and panel truck used to tow Miller's roadster and the snack stand to the lakes. Hal's dog is sleeping in the shade, under the front of his food stand.

In 1947, brothers Frank and Masao Morimoto of the *Mobilers* club brought out this Model A roadster. It was powered by a Ford Model B engine with a Cragar conversion and a supercharger. The supercharger is on the left side of the car and fed the intake manifold through a pipe than ran under the engine.

Because of the 1932 Ford's large frontal area, many competitors channeled the body to create a lower profile. Robert Clews of the *Oilers* club owned this 268-ci Mercury-powered roadster. In addition to the number on the side of his car, Clews painted a picture of an oilcan—the *Oilers'* logo.

The biggest car to run on the lakes in the 1940s was Charles Dimmitt's *Dimmittmobile*. Charles Dimmitt (standing in the center of the frame) built this orange-and-green behemoth over a three-year period from a Cadillac frame and a 1939 Lincoln Zephyr body. The engine, placed amidship, was a 1931 Cadillac V-16 that displaced 452 cubic inches. It was connected to two Cadillac transmissions, and one was reversed to increase the final drive ratio. The highest speed Dimmitt ran was a disappointing 110 mph, 20 mph off the D Roadster record. Dimmitt was a member of the *Autocrats* club.

One of the problems with any organization is the fact that at some point it becomes *large*. In 1948, the SCTA's members had to deal with huge crowds of spectators and long lines of cars waiting to compete. Many competitors looked elsewhere for a smaller group. This prompted the formation of several smaller timing groups. The smaller groups wanted to limit the organization's membership to 100 competitors from five clubs. The class structures were created so competitors had a chance to run more often. These small organizations lacked the long-term commitment of the SCTA, and they dissolved as quickly as they formed.

In 1948, the SCTA had over 500 active members in 31 member clubs. This was the largest the SCTA

One of the most consistent racers after the war was Phil Remington. When this photo was taken in 1947, Remington had applied a racy-looking two-tone paint job to his modified. Remington is seen fastening his helmet, a safety item that wasn't required by the SCTA until 1948. At the September 1947 SCTA meet, Remington set the B Streamliner record at 128.38 mph.

In 1948, Jack Avakian, a member of the *Road Runners* club, ran this red Model T roadster in the B Roadster class. Avakian installed a 1946 Mercury Flathead in the rear and added a streamlined nose to the front. The bucket seat was a surplus aircraft unit. On April 24, 1948, Avakian ran 128.02 mph at El Mirage. Inventive cars, such as Avakian's, challenged the expertise of the SCTA technical committee.

would ever be. Two things would simultaneously happen that would have a major impact on dry lakes racing—Bonneville and drag racing.

Off to Bonneville

Because of its large size and smooth surface, Muroc was the lake favored by racers. When the SCTA could no longer run at Muroc, it searched for another suitable dry lakebed. El Mirage was selected, but the SCTA officers knew that there must be something better. They spent countless weekends making road trips across Southern California and Nevada to find land speed's next mecca. They inquired about the prospects of access to Utah's Bonneville Salt Flats. Bonneville is

Elmer Chiodo of the *Outriders* club was like hundreds of other young Southern California men who built hot rods in 1947. His 1934 highboy roadster has a 1932 truck grille and light bar. A mildly modified Flathead is under the hood. Chiodo's wasn't the most beautiful car at the lakes, but he built it and had an opportunity to run down the lakes just like Stu Hilborn, Randy Shinn, and Phil Remington.

10 miles outside of Wendover, Utah. It was once a large lake that covered more than 19,000 square miles. Like the dry lakes of the Mojave, Bonneville's waters eventually evaporated and left behind a 150-square-mile saline residue that covered the southern end of the lake. The salt flats were first used as a race course in 1933 when Ab Jenkins, of Salt Lake City, drove his *Mormon Meteor* around a 10-mile circle and captured several long-distance records. In 1935, Sir Malcom Campbell had trouble getting his car up to speed on the sands of Daytona Beach and attempted to break a record at Bonneville. A 13-mile course was laid out with a 1-mile-long speed trap in the center. At 304.33 miles per hour, Campbell's first run was 27.51 miles per hour

The informal nature of dry lakes racing can be seen in this 1948 photo of the SCTA starting line. Racers and spectators mill about while Wally Parks fastens his helmet. The car Parks is standing next to is Bob Tattersfield's C streamliner belly tank. Tattersfield was a member of the *Road Runners* club. The gentleman behind Parks is Lou Baney. Standing across from the driver, smoking a cigarette, is someone who looks an awful lot like Ak Miller.

Art Lamey, driver for Bert Letner's "Elco Twin" C-class roadster, pulls up to the starting line at El Mirage. With its red-and-white paint scheme, this car was one of the prettiest on the lakes. In addition to running on the lakes, this roadster ran circle track races and was successful at both.

faster than what he had run in Daytona. On his return run, he only managed 297.93, but it was still fast enough to set an average speed of 301.13 miles per hour. This speed was well over the original, highly sought-after mark of 300 miles per hour. Campbell's run established Bonneville as the fastest and safest race course in the world. Hot rodders saw Bonneville as a legendary place where they could attain the highest possible speeds.

At that time, the American Automobile Association (AAA) had exclusive rights for the sanctioning of Federation Internationale de l'Automobile (FIA) record runs on the Bonneville Salt Flats. These were usually for foreign government-sponsored attempts for the likes of Campbell, John Cobb, Capt. George Eyston, and other members of the European elite. The reply the SCTA received from AAA was that the then-current Class C world record was 305 miles per hour and that it was "doubtful that any hot rod would ever reach that speed." Request denied!

The SCTA was insulted and persistent. In early 1949, Wally Parks contacted the Salt Lake City Chamber of Commerce. It was responsible for the recreational use of the Salt Flats. Parks defined the SCTA's qualifications and needs. He was invited to Salt Lake City to plead SCTA's case. "To add an amount of maturity and diplomacy to the venture, I enlisted Lee O. Ryan, senior member of the *Trend/Hot Rod* magazine executive staff, to accompany me in the presentation," says Parks. "As neither of us had transportation that we considered reliable enough for the journey, we invited Bob 'Pete' Petersen, *Hot Rod* magazine's founder, to come along with his 1939 Mercury club coupe." The three met with the Salt Lake City Chamber's secretary, Gus Backman. "Our reception was cordial and reassuring," says Parks. "After presenting the SCTA's record of accomplishments, and with Lee Ryan's support, we were given approval for a one-time 'trial' event. It was co-sponsored in 1949 by the

With minimal rules, dry lakes racers experimented a lot in the chase for more speed. This unidentified Model A roadster has a flathead installed in the back. While many experiments resulted in disappointment, some, like Tillborn's fuel injection and Burke's belly tank, proved to be revolutionary advancements.

SCTA and *Hot Rod* magazine as the Bonneville National Speed Trials—and the rest is history."

Drag Racing

Toward the end of 1938, the *Mobilers* club started timing quarter-mile runs that began with a standing start. Two of the members who ran modified roadsters ran the quarter in 14.5 seconds. Other clubs had also held quarter- and half-mile speed trials on an informal basis throughout the 1940s. The dry lakes racers wanted to race more than once a month and to race closer to home. "It [racing at the lakes] wasn't often enough," says Jim Nelson. "You got to run once a month, and the racers wanted to run every day. That's why drag

When drag racing became popular in the late 1940s, the impact was instantly felt at the lakes. Participation dropped because competitors could get the same level of excitement close to home in a cleaner environment. Here, the starter at San Diego's Paradise Mesa flags off a competitor.

racing took over." By the early 1950s, racers in Southern California could run two or three times a weekend. Drag strips were easily accessible location-wise, there wasn't dust to deal with, the temperatures were much cooler, and anyone who had a license and a car could race. Drag strips allowed any type of car to run. Instead of just roadsters and streamliners, Junior could take Dad's Oldsmobile Futuramic 88 down the strip. Soon the amount of people drag racing rapidly climbed over the amount of people who ever went to the lakes. Drag racing's popularity was verified in 1949, when the SCTA's attendance significantly dropped. Drag racing had the wheel-to-wheel spectator appeal that wasn't at the lakes.

Drag racing grew quickly, and drag strip owners saw that this type of racing could be a money-making business. Racers also realized that drag racing could be more than an amateur event. The SCTA and many other organizations sanctioned some early quarter-mile races. Under the direction of Wally Parks, the National Hot Rod Association (NHRA) was formed, grew, and prospered into the world's largest auto racing organization.

Although drag racing cut severely into dry lakes racing, drag racing owes much of its structure to the SCTA's basic rules. The initial classes, inspections, and course layout were straight from the SCTA rule book; the cars were classified by type and cubic-inch displacement. Many of the cars that raced on the lakes made a seamless transition to drag racing. Certain roadsters raced on the lakes, at the drag strip, and at California Roadster Association (CRA) circle track races with no modifications other than the tires.

While motor racing of all types flourished across the nation in the 1950s, dry lakes racing held its own. Its big disadvantage was its singular location. The unique track surface needed for high-speed time trials was impossible to duplicate anywhere else. The vast dimensions of the track also made it difficult to charge admission. Those who attended were subjected to the same dust, morning cold, and midday heat that had always plagued the dry lakes. Due to a hard-core group who loves the sport, dry lakes racing has survived. The SCTA still sanctions events on El Mirage each summer, and some of the same people who raced there in the 1940s still participate.

RACING AT
THE LAKES

Just prior to his run down El Mirage dry lake, Ralph Weston looks to his left and flashes a smile for the camera. He's wearing a leather flight jacket and one of the SCTA helmets that were loaned to competitors who didn't have one of their own. Weston's roadster is a 1929 Model A Ford powered by a 239-ci 1942 Ford Flathead. The engine was modified with Thickston heads, an Evans intake manifold, and a Winfield cam. The SCTA's starting line stand is in the background. Spectators were able to stand next to the cars as they left the starting line.

In order to race on the lakes, the drivers had to be fully committed to racing. The car had to pass technical inspection, and the driver had to belong to a member club of the sanctioning body. Club membership required working at an event in some support capacity. The commitment was confirmed if the driver could get to the lakes and endure the desert's harsh conditions. It was a long drive, the temperature was either brutally hot or icy cold, and the dust was never-ending. The thrill of driving a car as fast as possible brought the competitors there, as well as the technical challenge of learning how to go faster.

Early Preparation

Many hardy souls drove their cars up to the lakes, ran them as fast as they could, and then drove them home. Others towed their race cars. The amount of preparation required for the lakes depended on the type of car. Cars that were strictly used for competition, such as modified roadsters and belly tanks, received no special preparation other than the standard pre-race maintenance. The street roadsters that were driven to the lakes may have had a fresh set of plugs or a carburetor adjustment. Many of the street-driven roadster owners prepared their cars for the lakes a few days before the

Many racers would prepare their cars at home for competition and tow them to the dry lakes to race. This saved preparation time at the lakes and allowed racers to easily switch fuels from gasoline to alcohol. Photographer Don Cox took this photo in 1951 as he stopped to gas up his 1940 Mercury tow car on the way to El Mirage, where he ran his 1934 Ford coupe.

Bob Drew was a member of the *Low Flyers* and a regular SCTA lakes competitor. In 1947, he placed 22nd in points, which allowed him to place the number 22 on the side of his car for the 1948 season. Drew's 1932 roadster was a street-driven hot rod. It was also driven up to the lakes for competition where the headlights and windshield (now stored in the open rumble seat) were removed for racing. Drew's roadster was powered by a 1940 Ford Flathead with Lightning heads and an Engle cam. In July 1948, this car ran 122.79 mph at El Mirage.

event and towed them to the course. It was better to tow the race car than drive it to the lakes. If the car had a major mechanical failure during a race, the owner would have to find someone willing to tow the car home, usually on the end of a rope. Very few racers owned trailers. If a car were abandoned on the lakes after an event, "vultures" would pick it clean of any usable parts.

The preparation of a street-driven roadster for the lakes involved the removal of the windshield and headlights. This was an SCTA requirement. If the car had fenders, they also had to be removed.

Racers learned decades earlier that fenders acted like large, air-grabbing appendages that hindered speed. For additional power, many owners switched their fuel to alcohol for the lakes. This single change produced an instant 10 percent gain in horsepower. The use of alcohol instead of gasoline required larger jets in the carburetor because of the richer fuel mixture required. If alcohol were put into the car's regular gas tank, it would have to be drained, along with the fuel lines. Some competitors added a small, second fuel tank just for competition.

The drive to the lakes and then preparing a car to run was exhausting. This deuce owner is catching a little sleep on his female companion's shoulder while she reads the SCTA program. This roadster is trimmed with a custom instrument panel and a DuVall-style windshield. The windshield's glass panels have been removed.

Getting to the Lakes

Beginning in 1948, all SCTA events were two-day affairs that started early Saturday morning and ended on Sunday night. Serious competitors left for the lakes early on Friday to get in a few tune-up runs. Others made the three-hour drive after work on Friday night and arrived at the lakes in the dark. Some spectators would straggle in on Friday night so they could be awakened by the cackle of exhausts in the early morning and not miss a single run. Others simply showed up later in the day after racing had begun.

The drive to the dry lakes from Los Angeles was not an easy one. It was a lengthy drive over the San Gabriel Mountains. The road went from a few hundred feet above sea level in Los Angeles to slightly over 4,000 feet at the summit of the Cajon Pass. The ascent was steep and took its toll on the old cars that had marginal cooling systems. The climb was often made with one or more stops along the way to refill the radi-

ator. Jim Nelson's first trip to the lakes was made at night when temperatures were cooler. "We went up there at night," recalls Nelson, "because to get over Cajon Pass with an old Ford Flathead was unpredictable; it would overheat very easily. It took us two shots to get over Cajon Pass."

Towing a race car over Cajon Pass was even more difficult. Fred Lobello towed his 1932 roadster on many occasions. "I flat-towed it several times," recalls Lobello. "I remember one time a friend was towing me with his 1939 Ford sedan. We were going up Cajon Pass and we decided it was going to be too difficult to tow up the grade. So I got in the roadster and fired up the engine and helped push him up the hill." Once at the summit, Lobello climbed back in the tow car for the ride down the hill.

Lobello had a much more frightening trip to the lakes in 1946. "I was going to drive the roadster to an El Mirage meet and a friend offered to tow me in his

1940 convertible," says Lobello. He and the owner of the convertible hooked up the tow bar, which was made from a 1932 Ford wishbone. Because they were in a hurry, they didn't put a safety chain on the car. "Then this guy decided to take a girlfriend with him, so we had to have the top up. We were going through Santa Ana Canyon where the road was starting to go on the downgrade, and the ball on the hitch broke." When the tow bar fell to the pavement, it dug in and was torn off the roadster. Then the driverless roadster started to pass the convertible. "The car started to come by us and I wanted to transfer from the convertible to my roadster, but with the top up I couldn't get out fast enough." Lobello was partly out of the convertible when the roadster rolled alongside. The rear tire caught his leg, shredded his pants, and badly

bruised his leg. Lobello gave it another try and was almost all the way on the back of the roadster's seat when he saw it was about to leave the road. "I jumped back to the convertible and the roadster went into the ditch, flipped over, mashed the turtle deck area, and bent the radiator." Lobello's lesson learned was to use safety chains and never try to re-create the movie scene where John Wayne jumps on a horse to halt a runaway stagecoach.

The Summit, a restaurant located at the top of Cajon Pass, was where many racers stopped to have a cup of coffee. When they reached this point, the most difficult portion of the journey had been completed. "When you made it to that restaurant, it was downhill the rest of the way," says Jim Nelson. "You went in this restaurant, and here were all these guys you'd been

This is Fred Lobello's 1932 highboy roadster. It once came loose from its tow car en route to the lakes and ended up in a ditch. Lobello added a long collector pipe that ran along the right side of the car to run at the lakes. On the street, he used a split manifold with pipes that exited through the extended rear pan.

47

Approximately half of the competitors towed their cars up to the lakes for competition. A few had trailers, but most were flat-towed. Here, the Pierson brothers' 1934 coupe is being flat-towed by their beautiful 1936 Ford coupe. In addition to being a tow car, the coupe was also raced at the lakes. In 1948, at a Russetta Timing Association meet, the Piersons' 1936 coupe turned in a record time of 117.03 mph. It was also on the cover of the August 1948 issue of *Hot Rod* magazine.

reading about your whole life in *Hot Rod* magazine. They were really your heroes. They didn't know they were heroes, but in your mind, you'd made heroes out of them. They were sitting around talking and you just felt, 'God, I'm part of this group.' It felt bitchin' to be part of it." Nelson would soon be part of the lakes action. He never became a lakes hero, but he

later became one layer in drag racing as part of the Dragmaster team.

Jack Calori also stopped at that same restaurant when he towed his roadster to El Mirage. "When we got to the top of the Cajon Pass at a restaurant called the Summit, we would stop there and have some coffee, because it was generally cold," says Calori.

"Then I would break the race car loose from the tow car and I would drive the roadster toward Victorville." Calori was never shy when he opened up his roadster, and often cruised at over 100 miles per hour on the downhill run.

From the summit of the Cajon Pass, the route to El Mirage went through the city of Adelanto. This was the last place where food, cigarettes, or gasoline could be purchased. From there it's a short drive to the lake. All of the roads in that area are laid out on a north-south, east-west grid. The dirt road that leads onto the east-end lakebed is rough and filled with ruts. Once on the lakebed, the ride on the dry lake surface is unbelievably smooth. Arriving on the lake at night was a unique experience. For those coming out for the first time, it was difficult to locate the event staging area. Because the lakebed is so large and there are no defined roads or landmarks to help in finding one's direction, it was possible to drive in circles. When Jim Nelson and his friends first drove onto El Mirage at night, they were lost. "This was at night. The lake was just a great big flat area. The car's headlights would not go very far, because it was such a big black distance. We went tearing out across there, running around like a bunch of fools. The next morning there were people sleeping all over and cars parked all around. It was a miracle that we didn't run over somebody."

Competitors gathered at the far west end of El Mirage, where they parked their cars and set up camp for the night. Many people slept on the ground in sleeping bags, some brought surplus Army cots, and others slept in their cars. A few set up surplus Army tents. There were no designated spaces for the cars to park or for people to camp. Due to this lack of organization, many people were run over in the middle of the night as they slept. Other accidents happened on the lakebed at night when would-be racers opened up their cars and expected the lake to be perfectly flat in all directions with no obstructions or other cars to worry about. When Jack Calori ran for the first time at Muroc in the late 1930s, three people had been killed the night before. "They had no patrols in those days to keep you from running at night. It was very dangerous," says Calori. When Calori pulled up to the starting line to race in the morning, there were three dead bodies wrapped in white sheets. "I was about 16 years old and it sure did make you feel odd to look over and see three dead bodies before you started out on a run at Muroc."

Most racers camped overnight at the lakes, and they either slept in their cars, in sleeping bags on the ground, or in surplus Army tents. A Model A roadster is parked behind this radical-looking Model B–engined modified.

The nights on the lakes were very cold. Even in the midst of summer, the nighttime temperature on the lakes could drop into the 30s. Most people brought along plenty of blankets and warm clothing. Many built campfires to keep warm and to serve as a warning beacon for any cars entering the area. As dawn broke, activity slowly began. Everyone woke up to the rap-ping sound of open headers reverberating across the lakebed. People who slept in cars uncoiled from the confined space of a 1930s-era interior, and stretched to knock out the kinks in their back. Those with camp-fires would brew coffee and make breakfast. Most of the competitors wanted to shake off the cold and get their cars running as quickly as possible. A few would

A last-minute radiator check is done on Ray Brown's deuce roadster prior to a run. The hood on Brown's roadster is made of aluminum and filled with louvers. It also has an Eddie Meyer emblem on the side panel. The hood's top panel is tucked under the car while work progresses. The young man on the left is wearing what many people wore at the lakes: a Navy flight jacket, blue jeans with the cuffs rolled up, and engineer boots. The nights were bitterly cold, the days were brutally hot, and it was always dusty.

This sleek, channeled Model T roadster belonged to Randy Shinn. He won the 1946 SCTA points championship and set a two-way average of 126.58 mph with a one way speed of 132.74 mph. Shinn and Jack Calori had the two fastest C Roadsters in 1947. At the August meet, they raced each other in a special match race that Shinn won.

This Model A roadster may not have been the fastest or most beautiful car on the lakes, but it was obviously a chick magnet. The engine is fitted with Edelbrock heads and a dual-carburetor intake. The hood was a temporary addition to satisfy the SCTA's tech inspectors.

erect small tarps to shade themselves from the sun, in anticipation of the midday brutal heat.

"Oh boy, the nights were cold!" recalls Stu Hilborn. "If you've ever tried to start an engine on methanol in freezing weather, it's almost impossible. What I used to do when I was running carburetors was to take a quart can of benzene with me. Benzene would evaporate very easily. In the morning, before I started the engine, I'd pour a little benzene down the carburetor's throat, give the car a push, and it would generally start pretty good. It would run ragged until it got warmed up enough to where the alcohol would vaporize well. One night was particularly cold. I got up that morning and we got ready to put the benzene down the carburetor and, of all things, the benzene was frozen! So I had to melt the benzene first. The next time I came up I knew there had to be a better way. We always had a campfire because it was so cold. That morning we got up and the fire was out, but the coals were glowing. So I pushed the car so the engine was over the top of the coals. I let it sit there for about 15 minutes and then it fired up right away on the methanol."

Clothing

Because of the temperature extremes, an array of clothing was required for a weekend at the lakes. The nights required Pendleton wool shirts, sweaters, and jackets. In the daytime, T-shirts were the standard uniform. Even though it was hot, blue jeans with the cuffs rolled up were the trousers of choice. This was an era when men didn't wear shorts. At that time, tennis shoes were

Tom Beatty's 1927 Model T roadster ran 135.13 mph at the July 1948 SCTA meet. Channeled Model Ts were fast because of their light weight and small physical size. Beatty's engine was a 1932 Ford V-8 with Navarro intake and heads and a Weber cam.

only worn on the tennis court, so most men wore leather-soled shoes or engineer boots.

Following World War II, an array of surplus military clothing was available. Military clothing was inexpensive and extremely durable. Veterans also discovered that certain elements of their uniforms easily blended into civilian life. For example, Army khaki pants and Navy dungarees were common sights on the lakes following the war. Flight goggles and cloth flying helmets were very popular with drivers. The cloth helmet offered no protection other than keeping the driver's hair in place, but the flight goggles were excellent. The SCTA eventually required safety helmets and brought loaner models for those unable to buy their own.

Military flight jackets provided excellent protection from the cold. Each branch of service had its own

This engine was built by Barney Navarro, and he also built the blower drive and intake manifold. The carburetors are four Stromberg 97s that sit on top of a GMC supercharger. When run on a dynamometer, this engine produced 237 horsepower at 5,350 rpm. The addition of a supercharger to an engine bumped the car up one class on the lakes.

treatment of the venerable leather flight jacket. Most offered two versions—a standard model and a cold-weather edition with extra fleece lining. In addition to being warm and a great value at the surplus store, the jackets looked good. Military boots were popular because of their durability and low cost. Many veterans brought back a pair that were properly broken-in and comfortable. Ball caps, pith helmets, and stroker caps were worn for shade from the sun. Aviator sunglasses were also very popular. "We all wore Air Corps dark glasses," says Alex Xydias. "About 2 p.m., after running all day, you'd take the glasses off for a minute and—oh my God—it was so clear. You didn't realize how much dust had collected on them during the day until you'd take them off."

A few of the drivers wore white canvas coveralls because they offered an extra layer of protection from the cold, and they kept the street clothes underneath a little cleaner. "I wore a white pair of coveralls," says Fred Lobello. "We dipped them in a solution called 'sheep dip.' It was supposed to make them fire retardant." Luckily, Lobello never had to see if the solution worked. Many racers who wore coveralls had their club name emblazoned on the back. A few club members wore their club jackets with the club name and logo on the back. Clothing at the lake was strictly functional, with warmth, durability, and low cost as the key criteria in selection. No one went to the lakes to make a fashion statement—their car's performance was the reason they were there.

Food, Drink, and Diversions

To survive in the desert's hostile environment, both racers and spectators had to bring along plenty of water. Many treated a trip to the lakes as they would a camping excursion, and brought along a grill and food to cook. "I might take a sandwich or two, but I usually carried my barbecue," says Don Cox. "I'd buy a steak and cook it on the grill. If you quit early, you could start cooking at about 5 p.m. and go to sleep early." For those who didn't bring their own food, there were simple concession stands with a few basic items like sandwiches and cold drinks. One of the most popular vendors on the lakes was the ice cream truck. On a hot afternoon, nothing was more refreshing than an ice cream bar. Bill and Virginia Albright's Lazy A Ranch was on the north side of Mirage lake. They had minimal sleeping accommodations, a restaurant, plenty of

One of the best additions to SCTA's dry lakes events happened in early 1948 when public restrooms were brought to the lakes. The SCTA announced the addition in the April 1948 SCTA newsletter as being the first public restrooms in dry lakes racing history.

In order to run at an SCTA sanctioned event, you had to be a member of a club affiliated with the SCTA. The *Oilers* of Carlsbad, California, joined in 1948 and the members brought out their street Roadsters. This is *Oilers* member Jim Collin's channeled 1932 that reached a top speed of 109.48 mph. One of the many mobile food-vendor stands that would come out for the races is in the background.

Club Names

The SCTA and Russetta, the two largest dry lakes timing associations, were made up of member clubs. The individual members of these clubs supported and worked at the event and were thereby allowed to race their cars and receive an official timing. While the friendly rivalry between the SCTA and Russetta kept one club from joining both organizations (with the exception of the *Lancers*, *Dusters*, and *Gophers*), several individuals joined two clubs in order to race in both organizations' events. The member car clubs in the 1930s and 1940s had interesting names. Most were short, often one word, and they were usually automotive related. A few of the following clubs were in existence only a few weeks, forcing the members to move on to another organization. A couple of these clubs have survived, but most have passed quietly into hot rod history.

SCTA Clubs

Albatas	Mobilers
Almegas	Nite Owls
Autocrats	Oilers
Bungholers	Outriders
California Roadster	Pacers
Centuries	Pasadena Roadster
Clutchers	Quarter Milers
Desert Irons	Roadmasters
Detonators	Road Runners
Dolphins	San Bernardino Roadster
Dusters	San Diego Roadster
Gaters	Santa Paula Roadster
Gear Grinders	Serpents
Glendale Stokers	Sidewinders
Gophers	Southern California Roadster
Hornets	Strokers
Idlers	Throttlers
Lancers	Trompers
Low Flyers	Wheelers
Mad Mechanics	Whistlers
Milers	

Russetta Clubs

American Racing Club (ARC)	Prowlers
Arabs	Ramblers
Blow-Bys	Revs
Cam Pounders	Road Hogs
Cam Twirlers	Rod Riders
Choppers	Rodents
Coupes	Rotors
Drifters	Screechers
Dusters	Screwdrivers
Gazelles	Smokers
Glendale Coupe & Roadster	Stock Holders
Gophers	Taft Roadster
Hi-Winders	Throttle Merchants
Howlers	Turtles
Hutters	Velociteers
Lancers	Vultures
Lopers	
Moles	
Night Hawks	
Pan Draggers	

cold drinks, and a swimming pool. There was also the Rancho El Mirage that offered restrooms, cold beer, and free water. Restrooms were an important amenity because it wasn't until April 1948 that the SCTA installed the first public restrooms on the lakes.

On Saturday night and after the races on Sunday, a few of the guys would venture to Red Mountain and visit the local brothel. Red Mountain was on the edge of Edwards Air Force Base, which was a short drive north of Adelanto. "They always talked about Red Mountain," says Jim Nelson. "That's where all the hookers hung out. I don't know why the hookers hung out there, because there wasn't anything in either direction except for the military and miners."

The Course and Vehicle Inspection

As each racing season passed, the SCTA and other sanctioning bodies further improved the efficiency and safety of the meets. Initially, competitors and spectators parked wherever they wanted. The SCTA added a map to its program and designated certain areas for competition cars and an area for spectators, but there was no one to enforce the parking. The race course at each lake was generally laid out in a west to east direction. The prevailing winds (tailwind preferred) and any irregularities in the surface of the course were all taken into consideration. Because the lakebeds are so vast, the racecourse was never located in the same place twice. SCTA officials

This is Don Blair's 1927 Model T roadster kicking up dust at El Mirage and hitting at 114.50 mph. Blair's car was powered by a 286-ci Mercury Flathead, and it ran in the C Roadster class. Blair also owned Blair's Speed Shop in Pasadena, California.

In 1947, Jack Mickelson was a member of the *Gophers* club and drove this beautiful 1932 roadster. Every year the SCTA gave each club a block of numbers for its members' cars. In 1947, the *Gophers'* numbers ran from 144 through 162. Every car that competed was required to have its number painted on the side of the car. On September 21, 1947, Mickelson's roadster ran a speed of 129.31 mph at El Mirage.

selected the best piece of property on Friday, staked it out, and designated it with traffic cones. The distance from the start line to the beginning of the speed traps was 1.25 mile. The traps were exactly a quarter-mile long, and the shut-down area was 1.25 mile long. The return route to the starting line was on the northern side of the course.

Prior to the race, the cars were inspected to make sure they met the minimum safety requirements. Over the years, safety regulations became more and more stringent to protect the racers. In the 1930s, seatbelts and roll bars were not required. After the war, surplus aircraft seatbelts were readily available, and the SCTA made them a requirement. It would take several years before roll bars became standard equipment. Because most of the rear axles were Ford-manufactured with tapered ends, the inspector checked the cotter key. The inspector would also look at the steering gear and move the steering wheel from side to side to make sure the tie rod ends were in good shape. The competitor would have to remove the car's hubcaps so the lug nuts

and wheels could be inspected. Any car with cracked wheels or missing lug nuts would be rejected. It was a very basic inspection and few cars were rejected. Competitors were often able to fix any problem with their cars at the lakes and still be able to race.

All cars were required to have a hood of some type. This hood had to extend from the cowl to the radiator and around on the sides to the top of the vertical side panels. The side panels were optional. Many of the roadsters that were regularly driven on the street featured hastily assembled hoods that were attached with leather straps. These hoods weren't elegant, but they met the requirement in the rule book.

The inspector was also responsible for making sure each car had its assigned 12-inch-high number on both sides of the car. The numbers were assigned in blocks to each club and each competitor kept the same

number for the entire season. The exhaust was also inspected to ensure that the pipes were directed away from the lake surface to minimize the amount of dust stirred up. The exhaust pipes also had to be directed away from the driver's compartment and fuel system components. All cars were required to have a fire extinguisher mounted within the driver's reach. Cars that caught on fire were generally lost in the ensuing inferno. Although there was an ambulance on-site, there wasn't a fire truck around for miles.

Owners who drove their street-legal hot rods to the lakes transformed their vehicles into race cars on Friday night or Saturday morning. It was not unusual to see several full sets of fenders, headlights, windshields, and bumpers from a roadster in a pile at the edge of the lake. Highboy roadsters were easier to field-strip. The headlights and windshield

were the only items that had to be removed. Club members who parked together helped other members remove components and kept an eye on the parts during the event.

Running the Course

Once the inspector signed off the cars, they would form into lanes behind the starting line. Each car raced four runs a day, and each competitor had a card that was punched as he was about to make his run. Once a car was at the head of the line, the starter motioned

Left: This 1932 roadster scoots away from the starting line in a cloud of dust. Racing at the lakes was unlike drag racing, where a fast start and quick shifts were required for the lowest elapsed time. On the lakes, the starts were gradual, due to the tall rear-end gears, and all the shifts were easy.

The man behind the wheel of this 1932 roadster is Fred Lobello. He's smiling because he's about to make another run down El Mirage Dry Lake. His left hand is on the pump that supplies pressure to the fuel tank. He's wearing a helmet and a pair of military surplus goggles. The small piece of paper at the base of the steering column has speeds recorded for various rpms. The instrument panel insert is from an Auburn.

the car forward and held it at the line. Once the course was clear, the car was released for its run. The signal wasn't a wave of a green flag. It was a simple nod-and-hand motion. Most of the roadsters and coupes started on their own with little outside assistance. The streamliners and belly tanks required a push start. Because many of the streamliners were equipped with only a high gear, they chugged away from the starting line and took a while to build up speed. Roadsters and coupes equipped with transmissions would run through the gears. The drivers of the cars equipped with a tachometer would carefully watch the needle to prevent over-revving the engine. Jim Nelson didn't need a tach in his A V-8 roadster. "When you drive a car enough," says Nelson, "you know when to shift the thing. If you don't know when to shift, you shouldn't be out there running." Unlike drag racing, there is no hurry to get to the other end in dry lakes racing. It's

Thatcher Darwin's C streamliner was unusual. It was built on a Chevy frame and was powered by a 1941 Mercury engine. The body was listed in the SCTA program as a "Beetle," but it was probably hand-built or a cut-down production roadster. While Darwin adjusts his goggles in anticipation of his run, the line at the Swell Time ice cream truck grows.

As he passes on the left, the passenger in this roadster gives a quick wave to the 1936 Ford sedan's driver. They are on their way out of Adelanto, headed west for El Mirage dry lake. This area is known as the Mojave High Desert. It is inhospitable, but it's where the dry lakes are located, and that's where you can really open up the throttle and go fast.

Johnny Hartman transported his race car on a frail trailer. In 1948, this car ran in the Roadster class; but it was reclassified as a Lakester in 1949. It set the B Lakester record on May 8, 1949, with a one-way pass of 145.63 mph and an average speed of 140.09 mph. Hartman's 1927 Model T Ford was powered by a 248-ci Chevy six with a Wayne head and intake. Hartman was a member of the *Pasadena Roadster* club.

terminal velocity that counts, not elapsed time, so there was no need to speed-shift. As a result, there was very little transmission or clutch failure.

Each driver was on his own during the run, and cones marked the course. The lanes weren't marked, and there wasn't a centerline to follow. The only guides were the cones and the tracks left by the previous cars. "You just get it up into high gear and then settle down and ask yourself what's going to happen next," says Jim Nelson. "You're scared the whole time you're doing it. I never made a run with any race car that I was ever in that I wasn't a little apprehensive. I really liked it, but I was apprehensive. I respected the thing because I knew it could do me in if I screwed up."

As the run progressed, the driver would pump a little pressure to the fuel tank. Two or 3 pounds of pressure were all that was necessary to ensure the fuel was fed from the tank to the engine's mechanical fuel pump. This prevented the engine from being starved for fuel during the run.

As the car picked up speed, the driver positioned his head as low as possible. "I put my head down so low my eyeballs were just looking over the cowl," says Don Cox. Goggles were required in a car without a windshield. The faster the car went, the louder the wind noise would be for the driver. The drivers of front-engine cars, like most roadsters, heard the engine noise and wind. Belly tanks carried the engine

The young men working on this Model A roadster seem more interested in what's going on with the various cars on the lakes than they are with the otherwise provocative posture of the young female in the car. She has assessed the motives of the photographer and is making her feelings known.

Above: There were no rules in hot rodding in the 1940s. It was a time of unrestrained automotive experimentation. Ford products were favored for the body, chassis, and engine, but a few racers experimented with other engines like the Cadillac V-8 in this 1927 Model T roadster. Deuce grille shells were used on a wide variety of Roadsters. This one has been radically chopped to match the hood line.

Opposite: Dick Price of the *San Berdoo Roadster* club brought out this clean 1932 roadster to El Mirage in 1949. It featured a dropped front axle, hydraulic brakes, and tubular shocks. The front spreader bar has been smoothed into the ends of the frame rails, and the roadster has a custom-dropped front license plate mount. For anyone who wanted to build a hot rod, the lakes were a great place to see a variety of hot rods. Many hot rods were built with the high-quality workmanship of Price's roadster.

One of the biggest innovations to hit the dry lakes was the belly tank Streamliner. They were inexpensive and simple to build. This one was built by Bill Burke for the Lodes brothers. The driving compartment was cramped, but the view was great, and any mechanical problems were behind the driver.

in the rear and produced a different experience for the driver. "I heard the rear end more than the motor," recalls Alex Xydias. The rear end in his belly tank had straight-cut gears. "The rear end was just screaming. I remember that incredible screaming rear end." Belly tank drivers had the advantage of a small windshield in front of them to deflect the wind around their heads. Fred Lobello drove both a roadster and belly tank at the lakes. "In the Lakester with the windshield," says Lobello, "I couldn't tell I was going that fast."

The dry lake surface was hard enough to produce a squeal when the tires spun. As the car went through the course and gathered speed, the tires stirred up a fine layer of dust that covered the lake. From the

starting line, the car disappeared into the growing cloud of dust it created. Spectators who watched from the finish line first heard the sound of the engine, and then saw the tan-colored cloud. As the car approached, the high-pitched sound of an engine revving became louder and a speck of color appeared at the center of the cloud. Each engine—V-8, straight-eight, or four-cylinder—had its own unique timbre. The type of exhaust headers the owner had installed accentuated the sound. Soon, the dot in the center of the cloud was large enough to be recognized as a certain type of car. Roadsters running 1932 Ford grilles provided an extra audible treat for those near the traps. As the car reached approximately 90 miles per hour,

the grille produced a high pitched whistle attributed to the vibration of the grille's thin vertical bars.

Spectators and racers were able to have a good, long look at the cars on and around the starting line. They heard the engine as it idled and accelerated away in first gear. Those who chose to go to the area of the traps to watch the cars rocket by heard the engines at full song, and saw a huge rooster tail of dust kicked up by their tires. At one meet, Jim Nelson wanted to go down by the finish line to watch the cars go by at

Lakes competitors were willing to try anything in their quest for a faster mile-per-hour speed. Lewis Fergeson, a member of the *Albata* club, tried this unique set of exhaust headers in 1947. In addition to the opening in the rear, they had an opening in the front. His goal was possibly to use the ram-air effect generated by the speed of the car to help exhaust scavenging.

To maintain order at each dry lakes meet, certain club members were assigned patrol duty. Each person assigned received an armband and was asked to maintain crowd control. The patrol maintained the 20-mile-per-hour speed limit around the course and kept the crowd from getting too close to the cars during the races. This Lincoln Zephyr coupe, marked "Patrol" and sporting a red spotlight, is driving along the outside edge of the race course.

speed. It just so happened that he was able to witness history as Hilborn's streamliner, with Howard Wilson behind the wheel, ran the first 150-mile-per-hour speed ever recorded. "My memory of him [Wilson] going through at 150 miles per hour was seeing all the wheels slanted forward and there were streaks behind it, just like the old photos of the Indianapolis cars," says Nelson. "I thought 150 miles per hour—oh my God."

Running high speeds on the hard, crusted alkaline surface could be difficult. As more and more cars ran, the surface became covered in a layer of dust and was often referred to as being "soft." At low speeds, a car's

tires could drive through the surface dust. At higher speeds, the cars, especially the faster ones with high-horsepower engines, lost traction and started to fishtail. Tires hydroplane on dust just as they do on a water-soaked highway. "It was one of those days when the dry lakebed was not in good shape; it was soft," says Hilborn. "If you have enough power, and if the lakebed is soft, you lose traction and sometimes the rear end gets to fishtailing. Usually you can correct for it when you feel it." At the August 1947 SCTA meet, Hilborn lost traction when his streamliner came around. "I happened to look at the tach; I was just past 136 miles

per hour." Due to the speed of his car and the limited rear-end gear sets available, Hilborn used large 18 inch diameter wire wheels to attain a higher speed. When Hilborn's car went sideways, one of the rear wheel's wire spokes broke and the wheel came off. The axle dug into the ground and sent the car rolling. The only safety equipment Hilborn had was a seatbelt and advice from Indianapolis race veteran Eddie Miller. "Eddie Miller told me quite often that when they had problems in a race car at Indianapolis, they 'hit the cellar.' In other words, get down inside as low as you can, because we didn't have roll bars." As Hilborn's car rolled, the highest spot was his shoulders and back. "I

don't know how many flips I made, but there were several. I came out of it pretty good. I had two broken ribs here, and a large bruise on my back." Accidents like Hilborn's were the exception, and the majority of the cars had safe lake runs.

After the car crossed through the traps, the driver took his foot off the accelerator and let the engine's compression slow the car. There was over a mile where the car could slow down, make the turn to the left, and return to the starting line. Because of the long shutdown area, brakes were rarely needed. Rules didn't require four-wheel brakes, and many competitors ran only rear brakes. "You had to be careful shutting

A long racecourse requires a lot of communications gear and miles of wire. This young lad sits on the lake surface at the starting line and monitors the radio. Much of the gear used was surplus war material.

On the way home from the lakes, the driver of this hot rod stopped in Adelanto for something to eat. The youths in the Chrysler convertible are fascinated by the ragged 1934 Roadster.

down," says Bup Kettner, an *Oilers* member who ran an A V-8 roadster. "When you shut off, there was a lot of wind resistance on those old highboys, and you could slide around a little. If you tried to turn out too fast, it could be trouble. I would ease off the gas and I didn't do anything too extreme." Following the run, many of the drivers would hang out at the timing lights to see other cars go through.

The streamliners and faster roadsters would wait for their push car to come down to tow them back after they had stopped at the end of the run. Drivers would occasionally shut off the engine after they crossed the speed traps to get a reading off the engine's sparkplugs. The drivers would coast to a stop off to the left and pull the plugs to see if the fuel mixture was correct. Don Cox used the experience at the lakes to learn more about tuning. "I felt that we were running to learn," says Cox. "Every time I made a run, I pulled my plugs out to see how they were burning. Then I would adjust the jets, which was a simple project. If they were [Stromberg] 97s, you'd just pull two jet covers off the carburetor. If you kept track of all this, you learned something."

Racers who set fast times for their class during regular competition were allowed to make a "record run." Record runs were made at the end of the racing day and allowed competitors to set an official speed. A record run consisted of one run in the regular direction, quickly followed by a run from the opposite end of the course; then starting in the shut-down area, running through the speed traps, and slowing down and stopping as the driver approached the starting line. Running in the opposite direction was done to equal-ize any tailwind advantage the driver may have received on the initial run.

The Division of Labor

Anyone who wanted to become a member of the SCTA had to belong to a car club. At each event, each club was assigned tasks to help support the event. Because of the length of the course, the amount of race cars, and the number of spectators, there were many duties. One of the most important jobs was mobile patrol duty. The members assigned to the mobile patrol were the policemen of the meet. Their cars were marked with the word "Patrol," and they wore armbands to help distinguish them from the participants and spectators. The patrol's job was to contain the crowd. One of their main concerns were people who drove onto the racecourse. The patrol members also enforced the 20-mile-per-hour speed limit for vehicles not on the course. At this speed, the cars would not create a big cloud of dust. Spectators drove along the side of the course and could inadvertently create a large enough cloud to obscure the view of a driver on a high-speed run. The local sheriff's department or highway patrol would often supply a few officers to help.

There were many other important jobs at the dry lakes events. Assistants were needed at the starting line and finish stand. There were three signal posts along the course that required an attendant at all times when cars were running. There were miles of wire strung for communications that needed attention. A large clean-up crew was needed after the event was over. The many club members who worked the event and performed what may have seemed like minor, thankless tasks contributed greatly to the success of the events. They were the unsung heroes of the lakes who worked for free and didn't get their name in a record book. Most of the club members who were assigned to these minute tasks were newer club members, or those who didn't run a car that weekend.

Going Home

At the end of the weekend everything was covered in dust, especially the people, and everyone had too much sun. The long drive back to Los Angeles was easy because most of it was downhill to the L.A. basin. There were favorite diners and coffee shops along the way where weary racers would stop to stretch their legs and gather with their friends to bench race and swap lies. They would talk about how they would make their cars faster for the next meet.

CAR CLUBS
AND
SPEED SHOPS

The SCTA worked hard to enhance the image of hot rodding. On September 19, 1948, it gathered 300 club members from 36 clubs at the Lincoln-Mercury plant in Maywood, California. Here, the SCTA and its member clubs joined the National Safety Council. Each club displayed competition cars and street driven hot rods at the event.

The headlines in the Southern California papers were brutal: "Police Capture 31 Youths With Souped-Up Jalopies," "Jury Will Try Hot Rod Pair," and "Hot Rod Auto Crash Kills Two." Racing on the streets of Los Angeles was a problem in the late 1940s. One of the headlines in the *Los Angeles Times* in 1948, read "Judge Deals Out Jail Terms to 35 Hot Rodders." On March 3, 1948, 32 policemen surrounded and arrested 96 hot rodders who held a street race on Sepulveda Boulevard in the San Fernando Valley. The hot rodders and spectators created a blockade on Sepulveda that forced local residents to take a detour. The cars raced four abreast at speeds in excess of 100 miles per hour. Most were given tickets for minor violations, but Judge Joseph Call threw the book at 35 racers.

After he lectured them on the dangers of speed, he suspended their driver's licenses for 30 days and sentenced them to serve five days in jail. The offender with the longest list of charges was Willie Vega, who pleaded guilty to eight of the nine charges against him. This kind of bad publicity hurt hot rodding and reputable dry lakes racers, as well as race sanctioning organizations.

The SCTA always tried to promote safe hot rodding and waged a constant battle to receive positive press for hot rodders. Its motto was "Sponsors of the World's Safest Automotive Speed Trials." The SCTA enforced this motto and barred those convicted of traffic violations from association activities. Any repeat offenders were dismissed from the group. On September 19, 1948, the SCTA joined the National Safety Council at a large event staged at the Lincoln-Mercury plant in

Bob McGee's stunning red 1932 roadster was front and center at the SCTA/National Safety Council event. McGee bought the roadster in 1940. After he returned from the war, he rebuilt it into one of the finest hot rods of its day. McGee was a member of the *Gear Grinders* club.

Maywood, California, a suburb of Los Angeles. There were 300 club members from 36 SCTA clubs in attendance. They brought along 100 cars for display, which included everything from belly tanks to street roadsters. Ak Miller, then president of the SCTA, welcomed everyone and introduced George Prussel, head of the SCTA Safety Committee, who talked about the SCTA's commitment to safety on and off the track. Other speakers included representatives from the California Highway Patrol, the National Safety Council, and a Los Angeles municipal judge. The judge administered the National Safety Council's pledge to the SCTA members. The first car to receive a National Safety Council green cross decal was Bob McGee's red 1932 highboy roadster. This event was covered by all of the Los Angeles newspapers and *Hot Rod* magazine.

It was a big step to make the public aware that just because someone drives a hot rod, it doesn't necessary mean that he is a speed demon on the street.

The *Oilers* of Carlsbad, California

In order to become a member of a sanctioning body, a club had to apply. Once admitted, club members were allowed to run their cars under the sanctioning body's rules and help run the event. Many car clubs were formed shortly after witnessing an event on the lakes so they could go back and run. This was the case with the *Oilers* from Carlsbad, California.

After World War II, several veterans, and a few other friends who were interested in cars, hung out at the Apex Cafe in Carlsbad, just north of San Diego. Many were members of the government's "52/20 Club"

Three *Oilers* club members are checking out Phil Weiand's roadster at El Mirage. Jim Nelson, nicknamed "Conrad," is in the center of the group. The *Oilers* wore gold and purple-colored satin club jackets. These jackets were probably the most colorful of any club.

that provided $20 a week for 52 weeks to unemployed veterans. This separation bonus allowed veterans some free time to enjoy life. "We had a year's 'free gratis' from the government, so we went to the beach a lot and started hanging out in Carlsbad at the Apex Cafe," says Don Cox. "We were just a gang hanging out there. We all had cars and would go out and open the hoods and say, 'Look what I did.'" Initially, there were eight guys who were regulars at the Apex, and one day they decided to go to an SCTA lakes meet. Don Cox took his 5x7 Graflex camera and a 35mm camera with Kodak's new Kodachrome color film. "We did a lot of looking," says Cox. "The number one car at that time was a beautiful Model T roadster run by Randy Shinn. It was a really low, little buggy. I don't think he ever drove it on the street. We got excited and right then

and there decided to form a club when we got home."

The guys met at the Apex Cafe and talked about a name for their new club. "I think Jim [Nelson] suggested the name of the *Oilers* and we all agreed that it sounded great," says Cox. On one of the cafe's paper napkins, Nelson sketched out a logo to go along with the club's name. "We were all oily and greasy all the time, that's why you see the picture of the oil can with oil dripping out," says Jim Nelson. "We went to a war surplus store and they had a whole bin of these oil cans. So for the initiation to get into the *Oilers*, we put a chain on one of these oil cans and we made the guy wear it around his neck for a week. The guys did it if they wanted to be part of the *Oilers* club." The father of one of the members owned the Twin Inns in Carlsbad. He built the club a meeting room with a shower. "He [the father] said he

Part of the fun of being in a club is having your buddies around when you're building a car. Here, five *Oilers* club members gather at Jim Nelson's place to piece together a Model T. One member's chopped 1940 Ford is in the background.

was interested in getting racing off the street, but we were still doing it," says Nelson. In June 1948, the *Oilers* were the 37th club accepted into the SCTA. At that time, the *Oilers* had 20 members and 16 roadsters. Within two years, the club had grown to 50 members.

At each meet, the SCTA presented awards for the fastest cars in each class, and each car owner and club accumulated points for the year. The smaller clubs that were new to the sport, such as the *Oilers*, would have their own trophy presentations at the end of the year. These club award ceremonies, while small, were big events for the members and their wives and girlfriends. Officers of the SCTA attended these banquets and offered their support.

The *Knight Riders* of Fullerton, California

Fullerton, California's *Knight Riders* was one of SCTA's charter clubs. They had their first meeting on November 5, 1934. There were 19 young men in attendance, and they were all accepted as charter members. The common bond was good fellowship, an interest in building cars, and going on road trips as a group. By early 1935, the club's ranks grew to 34 members. The *Knight Riders'* rolling stock included eight roadsters, four sedans, and several coupes. The rapid growth attracted a few who were not interested in the original goals, and on May 18, 1935, the club was reorganized. The remaining 16 members were highly dedicated to the original goals, and they tried

Car clubs provided a support network at the lakes. There was always a buddy around to help remove the windshield and headlights. Often a car owner would return the favor by letting his fellow club members drive his car down the lake.

Although hot rod clubs of the 1940s were populated by men only, there were always girlfriends hanging around. They liked cars and imagined what it would be like to race down the dry lake bed. This young lady may have had dreams of being the next Veda Orr.

to recruit Roadster-only new members. In 1936, the *Knight Riders* sponsored three successful lakes meets at Muroc. In 1937, they sponsored meets at Muroc in conjunction with the *Tornadoes* from Santa Ana and Los Angeles' 90 *Mile Per Hour Club.*

Like many clubs of the era, the *Knight Riders* had a club plaque that every member displayed on his car. The member's speed rank within the club was on the plaque. The club had a difficult time regulating the numbers the members displayed. To settle the disputes, they all drove to Lucerne dry lake in June 1936, and raced to determine the official numbers. The club also devised a system where one member could challenge another member for his lower-numbered plaque. An official challenge had to be made at a regular club meeting, and it cost $1. If the challenger won, he exchanged plaques with the loser and his dollar was returned. If the challenger lost, 50 cents went to the one who had been challenged, and 50 cents went into the club's treasury.

The *Knight Riders* became one of SCTA's charter clubs in 1938. By 1939, the club had 19 active members and was in 10th place on SCTA's club point standings. Since its inception, the *Knight Riders* had taken 150 road trips that ranged from 25 to 700 miles, and sponsored seven dances and many parties. The dance they held on February 17, 1940, was reported in the March 1940 *SCTA Racing News* for garnering a profit of $3.20, and it was noted that everyone had a "swell" time.

The cars the *Knight Riders* owned contained a mixture of Cragar, Winfield, and Riley modified four-cylinder engines and several Flathead V-8s. All of the members wore black leather jackets with the club's emblem on the left pocket. In early 1940, the *Knight Riders* became known as the *California Roadster Club.*

The *Throttlers, Night Flyers,* and *Outriders*

The *Throttlers, Night Flyers,* and *Outriders* were all Los Angeles-area clubs that formed in 1937 and became members of the SCTA. The *Throttlers* were officially

78

organized on April 28, 1937, and met in a storefront clubhouse at 7714 Santa Monica Boulevard in Hollywood. Occasionally, late at night, the members would go over to Melrose Boulevard to race. The SCTA frowned on street-racing, but many of the *Throttlers'* members couldn't resist the urge.

At the time the club was formed, Pasadena's *Night Flyers* had 20 members. Its first trip to the lakes was for the SCTA's May 18, 1937, event. To become a member of the *Night Flyers*, an individual had to run 90 miles per hour, attend three meetings in a row, and receive 75 percent of the member's votes. The initiation fee was $1 and weekly dues were 25 cents. Each member was

also required to have at least one run timed by the SCTA each year.

Through the efforts of Lloyd Farmer, the *Omnibus* club was formed. The members met every Wednesday night at the rear of the Rio Grande Oil station at 5734 Santa Monica Boulevard. Within a year, the club had 25 members and boasted that none of them had received a traffic violation during that time.

The *San Diego Roadster Club*
In 1941, Fred Lobello worked at the Convair aircraft plant in San Diego. He owned a 1932 Roadster, but didn't know anything about the lakes or car clubs.

Ernest Graham of the *Lancers* club owned this Model A roadster. It has a 1932 Ford grille shell and a 1932 Chevy hood. A friend from the *Dolphins* club gazes at the Flathead engine. He's wearing white coveralls with the *Dolphins'* logo on the back.

In the 1940s, hot rodders were seen as hooligans and troublemakers. This guy's neighbors were probably not too pleased to see these four hot rods parked in front of the house. The SCTA constantly reinforced the notion that hot rodding was respectable and safe.

Car club plaques were cast out of aluminum that featured the club names and logos. If they were SCTA members, that information was proudly added to the plaque. This little Model A roadster has a *Road Runners* club plaque, designed and produced by Wally Parks, to the right of the license plate.

Lobello met John Cerveny at the plant, and through Cerveny, he was introduced to the newly formed *San Diego Roadster* club. Lobello attended a few of the club's functions and converted his roadster to a highboy. The club would often meet with other Los Angeles-area clubs for picnics or a little racing. "On Sunday May 14, 1944, we went up to Temecula [California] and met a lot of the *Road Runners*," says Lobello. "We got on a country road and did some drag racing." Otto Crocker set up his clocks and the cars ran from a standing start. "I would say that we took part in one of the first drag races." Upon his return from military service, Lobello accompanied the club to a lakes meet sponsored by the Pacific Coast Timing Association. On September 12, 1945, he was voted into the club and has been a member ever since. The *San Diego Roadster* club is still

active today and its members regularly participate at lakes meets.

The *Sidewinders* of Glendale

The *Sidewinders* is one of the oldest hot rod clubs in existence. In 1937, the *Sidewinders* was formed by a small group from Glendale, California's Hoover High School, and met at Bob's Drive-In in Glendale. In 1938, then called the *Glendale Sidewinders*, it became one of SCTA's charter clubs. The members competed at the lakes, but they never had the success that some of the other clubs and their members enjoyed. "The *Road Runners* were the big kings," recalls Alex Xydias. "They had Ak Miller, Randy Shinn, and Wally Parks, and they were the points champion." Xydias belonged to the *Sidewinders*, whose club points standings were

Reliability Runs

In the formative days of hot rodding, clubs used to stage reliability runs to prove a home-built hot rod's endurance and a driver's skill. These runs were designed to be a road competition during the winter off-season. One or more clubs hosted the reliability runs. These runs were more than a drive in the park, and because of their complexity, they took considerable planning.

Long before the day of the run, those responsible for the event established a route, selected locations for checkpoints, then surveyed and charted the times and distances. There were a variety of roads and driving conditions within the 100-mile route. The reliability runs organized in Southern California included mountains, deserts, and cities. Once the route was finalized, the organizers created a map that showed the locations of the check stations, as well as the distance and average speed that had to be maintained between the check stations. Maps were printed and distributed to each competitor on the day of the run. Sponsoring club members canvassed local businesses for donations of goods and services as prizes. Entry blanks were mailed to members of the host club(s) and to members of other clubs in the area. A few days prior to the run, one of the organizers visited the law enforcement agencies that had jurisdiction of the streets and cities within the course. The last item was the assignment of club members to man the route's checkpoints.

The day of the reliability run started early for the organizers. Those assigned to checkpoints were in place long before the first car was turned loose. Competitors also lined up early to be one of the first to run the course. At the assigned starting time, the official starter sent the first competitor on his way with a map of the course and a few basic instructions. The balance of the competing cars was released at 1-minute intervals. The object for each driver was to cover the distance between the checkpoints at the time surveyed by the organizers. Each car was marked with a large entry number on its right-hand door. As each car passed a checkpoint, those at the station noted its time. At the midpoint of the run, a 20- or 30-minute layover would be scheduled to allow competitors to grab a quick lunch and top off their gas tank. Often, a hidden checkpoint not on the map was added to the course. These were added to keep competitors on their toes. At one run co-sponsored by the *Pasadena Roadster* club and the *Pasadena Pacers*, SCTA timer Otto Crocker set up his clocks at a hidden location to monitor speeds. Points were charged against those who exceeded the speed limit. At a rate of one point per minute, points were added for arriving at a checkpoint too early or too late. Points were also added to those who received moving violations during the run. A perfect score was zero.

After the last car was released from the starting line, a chase vehicle followed. That driver and passenger let those at the checkpoints know that the last car had passed. The run usually ended at the same location as the starting point. Once the last car arrived, the points were tabulated. Some of the distant checkpoints called in their results from a pay phone to speed up the process. The driver with the fewest penalty points was designated the winner. The true winners were everyone who finished without a breakdown and proved that their home-built hot rods were reliable.

Sometimes going to the lakes meant hauling fuel and tools for a fellow club member instead of racing a car. This slick Model T roadster pickup could have run in the Roadster class, but its bed was filled with fuel cans.

dismal in comparison to those of the *Road Runners*. "We were like dead last, so I said, 'We're going to beat the *Road Runners*.' " Xydias started a campaign to recruit new members with faster cars. He also played fast and loose with the rules. Central California car customizer Gene Winfield was a customer at So-Cal Speed Shop and a friend of Xydias. He had a quick roadster and Xydias had him come down and run under the *Sidewinders'* club banner and used the name of a member who didn't have a car. "Winfield's still got the timing tag for 'Joe Blow,'" laughs Xydias. Xydias recruited two other belly tanks with V-8 60 engines. Along with his belly tank, this trio of cars garnered first, second, and third at every SCTA meet they ran. "I stole Ray Brown from the *Road Runners*," says Xydias. "That was

the biggest political brouhaha ever! We beat the *Road Runners* and became points champs in 1950."

The clubs were the foundation of the SCTA and other sanctioning bodies that raced on the lakes. They also played a significant role in producing a lakes event. The clubs were where the guys got together on weekends to talk about cars and racing when there wasn't a lakes meet. It was also a social scene and clubs would host dances and picnics. The clubs provided an organization for young men to belong that offered brotherhood, an environment where people with similar interests could meet, and a setting where one could learn from others about the mechanics of cars. The car club was a place to find a mentor who would be willing to teach a new member how to jet a

Paul Schiefer was a member of San Diego's *Southern California Roadster* club and ran this beautiful, blue 1925 Model T roadster in 1948. When it appeared at the first SCTA meet in 1947, it was judged the Best Appearing Car. The flywheel also exploded at the meet. On July 18, 1948, Schiefer's C roadster ran through the clocks at a speed of 148.02 mph.

Stromberg carburetor for alcohol or how to port and polish. The dry lakes sanctioning bodies required clubs for participation. Once the sport of drag racing took hold, many of the clubs disbanded because there were no club membership requirements to compete at a drag strip. However, the SCTA has held fast with its rules regarding club participation, and some of the original clubs are still active in lakes competition.

Speed Shops

The 1940s saw the rapid growth of speed shops. These shops were not auto accessory stores that sold a few high-performance items. Speed shops were where you went to get manifolds, heads, and cams that were not

Hare & Hound Run

One of the most popular car club events in the 1930s and 1940s was the Hare & Hound Run. At this event, a club member (the "hare") drove a course through the club's neighborhood or city. He marked the course and dropped a sack of lime or flour in the center of any intersection where he changed direction. The hare would turn and drop another sack approximately 200 to 300 feet from the intersection to mark the direction. After the course was marked, the hare would drive it at the legal speed limit and determine the minimum time needed to complete the course. This would be the benchmark time all competitors (the soon-to-be-released hounds) had to stay within.

The event began when the "hounds" (club members driving their car with a buddy, wife, or girlfriend as navigator) were released from the starting location at 2- to 3-minute intervals.

The hounds approached each marked intersection and had to guess which direction they needed to drive. If a hound turned right and didn't see another sack of lime in the road, he'd have to double back to the intersection because the hare had gone left instead of right. As you can imagine, this event generated a lot of fun and hilarity as drivers made tire-smoking U-turns throughout the city, avoided collisions with other hounds, and pushed the edge of the speed limit. The hound that completed the course with the time closest to the one run by the hare won a prize.

Entry fees were usually 10 cents, and the winning hound took the majority of the money collected from the other hounds. The end of the course was usually a scenic park where the entire club could relax and enjoy a picnic.

available at regular auto parts stores. The smell of parts cleaner and gasoline permeated speed shops. Racing trophies were proudly displayed, and calendars featuring photos of scantily clad women hung on the wall. Shelves were stocked with the latest manifolds and cylinder heads. It was a place where men smoked cigarettes, laughed raucously, and punctuated their sentences with profanity. Speed shops were magical places to hang out. It was possible to eavesdrop on a conversation between dry lakes heroes talking about cam lift, carburetor jets, or ignition timing. Most novice hot rodders just looked and listened. Those willing to ratchet up their courage to talk to one of these men would find that they were a wealth of knowledge and usually more than willing to share their expertise. This was the place to get advice on how to

make your car go faster; that kind of advice was not available at the average auto parts store.

Alex Xydias was determined to open a speed shop when he returned from World War II. "I was interested in cars, I had this beautiful little Cabriolet that I was proud of, and I wanted a speed shop," says Xydias. There were several high-performance auto parts stores in the Los Angeles area at the time, but he recalls the impact that the words "speed shop" added to Karl Orr's Speed Shop. At the end of the war, with so many young men being discharged, there was a backup of paperwork. Xydias spent two months at home waiting for his discharge. "I had two months to look for a building, rent it, and build the shelves," says Xydias. "I could do all that because I didn't have anything else to do. I was still in the service." He decided that his

Kenny Yenawine was a member of the *Southern California Roadster* club, and drove this beautiful 1932 roadster to speeds of just under 120 mph. Yenawine's low seating position kept him out of the high speed wind stream while he raced on the lakes. This seating position also became fashionable for hot rodders when they cruised on the streets of their communities.

hometown of Hollywood wouldn't be the best place to open a speed shop, so he traveled to Burbank. He found a small storefront for rent on Olive Avenue. Xydias had a few of his friends, who were also veterans and unemployed, help him fix up his new shop.

In 1946, Xydias opened the So-Cal Speed Shop and parked his beautiful 1934 Cabriolet in front of the store. "My best friend today was my first customer," says Xydias. "He saw my Cabriolet out in front and came in. I had never seen him before, and by the time

he left we were best friends—it was one of those rare things." Xydias stocked the shelves with mostly bolt-on accessories like chrome acorn nuts to dress up Flathead engines and Stewart Warner gauges. "I think the guys wanted to get their car first and then do a few things to make it look better." Xydias also looked for bargains at the local surplus store where he bought seatbelts and goggles. One of Xydias' best sellers was the 16-inch steel wheel. "I was good friends with the Ford agency in the area," says Xydias. "They would call

Left: Because of Southern California's temperate weather patterns, it was possible to drive a roadster year-round. This blue 1929 Model A is mounted on a 1932 frame. It features a Flathead V-8 engine, chrome, and a DuVall-style windshield.

Below: In 1947, photographer Don Cox stopped alongside the Pacific Ocean to shoot his 1932 roadster. Cox ran both roadsters and coupes at the lakes, and he always felt the roadsters were the "real" wind-in-the-face race cars. This roadster was eventually painted yellow. Chrome wheels were a rare addition in 1947. Cox was a member of the *Oilers* club and organized several of the *Oilers'* Hare & Hound Runs.

me when they got in a shipment of steel wheels, and I'd go buy every one of them." As quickly as he could stack them up in the shop, they were sold. Kelsey-Hayes wire wheels had been a popular alternative to a stock Ford wheel, but the 16-inch steel wheels with hubcaps and beauty rings were the look everyone wanted in the late 1940s.

Another one of Xydias' early friends and customers was Dean Batchelor. He was also drawn into the shop by Xydias' Cabriolet parked in front. Batchelor drove a 1932 roadster every day and occasionally raced it at the lakes. Xydias used Batchelor's roadster to advertise his new business. "We took Bon

Ami and wrote 'So-Cal Speed Shop' on the cowl," says Xydias. Batchelor's Roadster was the first car sponsored by So Cal Speed Shop. Xydias also advertised in the SCTA and Russetta race programs, and put flyers on the windshields of cars at the local midget and Roadster races. "The midgets were huge, every night there was a midget race somewhere," says Xydias. After advertising to so many racers, Xydias realized he had to do more than just sell speed equipment. He had to race.

To get into racing, Xydias moved to a building where a race car could be worked on and stored. "After a year, I left that little building on Olive and got a lot

An easy way to find Alex Xydias' So Cal Speed Shop on Victory Boulevard in Burbank was to look for his black 1934 Cabriolet—it was always parked in front. This young gentleman admires Xydias' car. Speed shops were the place to go to get the latest parts and information.

In the 1940s, hot rodding was seen by most people as a dangerous and irresponsible activity. Car clubs organized hot rod shows to show the public what could be done with an old car. This show took place at a paved circle track, and the cars lined up along the main stretch.

on Victory Boulevard. I put this Sears prefab, two-car garage on the lot. All my friends were in construction and we put that thing up in no time at all," says Xydias. One thing that Xydias forgot to do was install a rest-room in his new building. "The inspector didn't notice that this commercial building didn't have a restroom, and I didn't notice either." Luckily there was a drive-in restaurant on the corner and its restroom was across

the alley, so the guys from the shop didn't have to go in the restaurant to use the restroom.

After Xydias built a belly tank streamliner, it was parked outside the shop every day to attract new customers. Jim Nelson was new to hot rodding after the war. "We'd get in the Roadsters and drive up to L.A. and go to So-Cal or anyplace that might be open," recalls Nelson. "Gas was only 20 cents a gallon. We

2820 UNIVERSITY
PHONE W-0617

SPARK PLUGS · TIRE PUMPS · WHEEL DISCS · FLEX TUBING · GAS CAPS · SEAT COVERS · MUFFLERS · JACKS

wanted to be part of hot rodding. We'd go in the front and look around. They wouldn't let us go in the back. We were just dumb kids. We weren't smart enough to know what to ask these guys."

Speed shops were magnets for neophyte hot rodders. These shops in the L.A. area fostered the growth of hot rodding throughout the 1940s and 1950s. They were places where experts developed new speed techniques and novices learned the basics. They were also a place to hang out, see the latest cars, and meet the future legends of hot rodding.

Speed shops were not on every corner, even in Southern California. Most parts were either scrounged from junkyards or bought at a local auto parts store. This roadster's owner has parked his car and crossed the street to his local auto parts outlet.

DRY LAKES
ROADSTERS

This 1932 Ford was typical of the roadsters that were driven on the streets of Southern California and the dry lakes in the late 1940s. It features a custom paint job, filled grille shell, chopped windshield, and a finely tailored top with side curtains. The highboy roadster style with big-'n'-little tires was born on the dry lakes.

Roadsters had been popular as race cars as far back as the 1920s when Model T races were run. The roadster was the mainstay of the lakes racers, and with the exception of streamliners, it was the only body style the SCTA allowed to race for several years. Roadsters were faster than a comparably powered coupe because the windshield could be removed for a distinct, aerodynamic advantage. Roadsters were inexpensive and plentiful in Southern California, especially after the war. The favored combination was the "A V-8," a Model A Ford roadster body with a Flathead V-8 engine. Model Ts were also converted to V-8 power. There were a lot of 1932 roadsters, and a few 1933 and 1934 models ran at the lakes. These later models came from the factory with a V-8 and were the easiest to convert to a more powerful Flathead. They were also larger, which contributed to wind resistance, and therefore were slower.

While the 1933 and 1934 Ford roadsters were not popular with lakes racers, the coupes became legendary.

When Henry Ford built the Model A and the 1932, he probably didn't realize they were going to be raced as much as they were. One reason for their popularity was that parts were easily interchangeable with Ford components. The clutch housing's bolt pattern for the transmission on the 1932 V-8 was the same in 1948. Therefore, a transmission from a 1948 Ford would fit right into a 1932. Ford didn't change the basic design very much, everything was very easily interchangeable, and parts were cheap. Anyone, especially after the war, could go to a wrecking yard and find axles, transmissions, and complete engines. Although wages were low, the basic Ford car and bolt-in wrecking yard components were inexpensive.

Most of the lakes competitors used bolt-on components to increase horsepower. Few people knew how to

Jack Morgan was a member of the *Clutchers* club. In April 1948, he brought his red 1934 Ford roadster to the lakes. It was powered by a 1941 Ford Flathead with Meyer heads and a Navarro intake manifold. Due to their size, these big 1933 and 1934 Ford roadsters were not commonly raced.

Smiling Ed "Axle" Stewart was a well-liked hot rod pioneer who drove this beautiful 1932 roadster. He earned the nickname "Axle" because his business manufactured the first dropped-front axles. The axles became known as "dago" axles, named after Stewart's hometown of San Diego. His 1932 roadster featured chrome backing plates on the brakes, a custom-louvered hood, and custom farings on the door hinges. Stewart's C-class roadster was powered by a 1941 Ford Flathead with Evans heads and intake and a Weber cam. On July 18, 1948, Stewart clocked a speed of 128.93 mph in this roadster at El Mirage.

tear down an engine. Money was scarce, and whatever parts were purchased had to be easy to install, add performance, and increase visual appeal. Multiple carburetors, high-compression heads, and exhaust headers were the most common modifications. Cams were available, but understanding them was tricky, and successful installation was beyond the mechanical reach of most competitors. Ignition systems were also mysterious, and most racers made a simple change to a hotter coil. For the racers who rebuilt their engines, pistons and rings were inexpensive and easy to obtain. Stronger valve springs from Lincoln Zephyrs were often installed, and a few competitors made a mistake

and used larger intake valves as exhaust valves. The intake valves were not designed to handle the exhaust's heat, they stretched, and provided a built-in governor. Carburetors, mostly Strombergs, were plentiful and easy to rebuild. The racers whose cars ran on alcohol found it easy to modify the carburetors. A hand-operated pump was added to pressurize the fuel tank and keep the engine from being fuel-starved on a long, high-speed run. Pumps were standard equipment on full competition roadsters and were installed on most street roadsters that regularly ran at the lakes.

Chassis and suspensions were a mix-and-match of basic Ford parts. Ed Stewart's dropped "dago" (a shortened

This young lady is bundled up to keep warm on a cold El Mirage morning. She is keeping track of this 1927 Model T Ford roadster. The custom headlight bar is a good indication that this car was regularly street-driven. Its whitewall tires were a rare commodity after the war; the front pair features two-sided whitewall motorcycle tires. Other interesting features include the chopped 1932 grille shell, a custom hood with smooth sides, and a 1940 Ford steering wheel.

version of San Diego, Stewart's hometown) axles were popular after the war. This axle gave the car a lower front profile. Beginning in the late 1940s, most of the street-driven machines switched from mechanical to hydraulic brakes. Roadsters designed strictly for competition used only rear brakes. This may sound dangerous, but there wasn't a need for heavy-duty brakes. Once a roadster ran through the traps, the shut-down area was so long that a car could have easily raced

without any brakes at all. Prior to the war, wire wheels were common. The best replacements for the weaker Ford wire wheels were Kelsey-Hayes wire wheels. After the war, the 16-inch solid steel wheels became popular and competitors ran with hubcaps and beauty rings. Most of the roadsters used street tires. Gearing was limited, so everyone who ran roadsters ran larger-diameter rear tires. This numerically lowered the rear-end ratio and allowed higher top speeds. A few competitors bought used Indianapolis tires. These were larger in diameter and could easily handle the speed of a lakes roadster. Tread was important to obtain traction on the lakebed, especially if it was soft. Competitors used several different methods (the most laborious was a hacksaw) to cut extra grooves in their rear tires for additional traction.

The most popular roadsters at the lakes and on the street were the A V-8 and 1932. An A V-8 is a 1928 or 1929 Model A Ford roadster with a Flathead V-8 engine. The A V-8 used either the original Model A frame or one from a 1932 Ford. The Model A body fit nicely on the 1932 rails and provided a stronger chassis than the original Model A frame. Ford produced a Model A roadster in 1930 and 1931, but the body style changed slightly and never had the appeal of the 1928 and 1929 models. A few were run, but most stuck with the 1928 and 1929 models. Almost every A V-8 sported a 1932 Ford grille shell.

The 1932 Ford roadster was the quintessential dry lakes hot rod. Its classic lines had an enduring quality that was attractive to hot rodders. The styling was refined, and in stock V-8 form, the car was as fast as any production car on the road. Any Ford produced in 1932 eventually became known as a "deuce," which referred to the number "2" in its year of production. In the 1940s, the 1932 Ford was an inexpensive used car. Many postwar young men easily turned it into a hot rod. The switch to a later, more powerful Flathead was simple. Ford's 1940s-era production cars had upgraded chassis components, including transmissions, rear ends, and hydraulic brakes, that were easily swapped into the 1932. Dry lakes racers loved the deuce because the fenders and running boards could easily be field-stripped for competition. On the street, the 1932 looked good with or without the original fenders. For more variety, the roadster body could be channeled down over the frame rails to provide a lower profile with less wind resistance. Popular modifications to the body included removal of the ornamentation and radiator filler on the grille shell, smooth-sided hood panels, and 1939 Ford teardrop taillights.

Other notable lakes roadsters were the Ford Model T, and 1933 and 1934 Ford. The Model Ts were the smallest and offered the least wind resistance. The most serious racers, such as Harold Daigh, Doug Hartelt, Randy Shinn, and Paul Schiefer, used these bodies. The smaller T roadsters were popular on the

This Model A roadster, owned by Art Tremaine of the *Strokers* club, features a highly polished custom aluminum hood. The chrome headlight brackets and hydraulic brakes are two good indications that this car was driven on the street. Chromed hairpin radius rods are another custom feature.

Above: Wally O'Brien of the *Strokers* club raced this clean 1932 roadster at the lakes. On April 25, 1948, he ran a speed of 125.87 mph at El Mirage. O'Brien filled the car's grille shell and removed the door handles. He also removed the windshield, and left the stanchions in place. He added a red vinyl tarp over the passenger compartment to reduce drag for the lakes runs. In the distant background are three private airplanes that have landed on the lake.

Left: The owner of this 1932 roadster has taken a lot of time to detail the custom stainless instrument panel in a finish called "damascening," which is also known as engine turning. A full complement of gauges is spread across the panel, and a 1940 Ford steering wheel and column shift have been added. The glass has been removed from the DuVall-style windshield in anticipation of a run on the dry lakebed.

Brothers John and Bill Eppard of the *Pasadena Roadster* club built this unusual roadster that they ran in 1948. It features a 1929 Model A body and frame with a 212-ci four-cylinder Ford Model B engine. Because of the driver's position and the extended wheelbase, it is obviously a mid-engine arrangement. The body is stock, but some streamlining has been added below the grille shell, as well as some side skirts.

CRA (California Racing Association) circuit. These roadsters would often do double duty and race on a dirt oval track one day, and race on the lakes the next. In 1933, Ford redesigned its passenger cars with a more streamlined, but larger car. This design carried over into 1934. The 1933 and 1934 Ford roadsters were seen as too big and heavy for lakes racing, but a few competitors raced them. Besides the Fords, there

were a few competitors who ran other manufacturer's roadsters. The most successful was the Spurgin & Giovanine 1925 Chevy.

Jack Calori's Roadsters
When Jack Calori was in high school in the late 1930s, he found a 1932 Ford roadster he wanted to buy. The roadster's hood had solid side panels, a beautiful, black

Jack Calori bought this A V-8 roadster while he was in the Navy during the war. It was his only means of transportation for several years. On this trip to the lakes in 1946, he ran the engine for someone who wanted to see how fast it could go. Calori had to add a temporary hood in order to race. His roadster ran 104 mph with this engine. Later in the year, he installed his own engine and reached 120 mph.

paint job, and a nicely trimmed interior. The price was $200 and Calori had the money. While he was in a café with his mother, he described the car to her and looked for her approval to make the purchase. "I wanted to buy that car," says Calori. "She said, 'No, you're not going to have a car like that.' I told her, 'I'm going to build one!' She laughed, and so did the man who was waiting on us." Calori went to the Alameda wrecking yard in Los Angeles and bought a 1926 Ford frame and 1926 T body. "I can't remember what I paid for the

Jack Calori's A V-8 roadster had one of the most beautiful sets of pipes ever installed on a lakes roadster. They exited a custom-blistered hood built by Herb Renau. Renau welded the doors shut and smoothed the sides. The interior upholstery on Calori's car was Spanish red leather.

frame, but the body had perfect metal and was only $2." Calori bought a 1924 Chevy engine with a three-port Olds head for $15 from Jim White's Speed Shop. "I was worried that the engine wouldn't run," says Calori. "I was assured that it would, so I went ahead and built the car." Calori's lack of tools and car building experience was overcome by his enthusiasm and energy. The car had a Model A hood, 1932 Ford grille, and 1938 Chevy wheels with large rear tires. "I built this car, and it was fast and beautiful," boasts Calori. "It accelerated very fast. The only problem was the oil pump." The engine had a Jewet oil pump that ran off the camshaft. Due to vibration, the pump quit and the engine failed. Calori had the engine rebuilt and traded that car for a 1929 Ford with a Winfield head and Winfield SR carburetors. "I ran four pipes out the passenger side into a 3-inch collector pipe," says Calori. "I ran that car at Muroc. It went 101 miles per hour, which in those days was presentable." Calori then

bought a 1932 roadster that he also ran at Muroc. The war soon put Calori's lakes racing on hold.

The roadster that Calori is most famous for is his black A V-8 with long chrome pipes. It was a car he picked up and drove while stateside in the Navy. "In April 1946, I bought a brand-new 1946 Merc engine and I split the wishbones," says Calori. He had the engine bored 1/8 inch and stroked 1/8 inch. It had a Weiand intake manifold with two two-barrel Chandler & Grove carburetors, Eddie Meyer heads, and an ignition that utilized a Lincoln Zephyr coil. Calori worked part-time for cam grinder Clay Smith, who ground him a special cam. Smith advised Calori to take the flywheel clear down to nothing. When Calori was finished with the aluminum flywheel, it weighed 4 1/2 pounds and allowed the engine to rev like a kitchen blender. There was just enough edge distance on it for the pressure plate and no starter ring gear. Without a ring gear, the car had to be push-started. Calori installed Lincoln Zephyr gears in a Ford box. Once the car was ready, Calori took the roadster to Smith's shop in Long Beach. "Clay jumped in the roadster and ran down the street; naturally a cigar was hanging out of his mouth. When he returned, he said, 'Jack, that's a 120-mile-per-hour car!'" Calori was impressed that Smith thought the car was that fast, because in 1946, 120 miles per hour was a very good speed. On Calori's first trip to El Mirage with the roadster, he ran 119.86 miles per hour, and backed up Smith's prediction.

Calori's A V-8 was his daily driver. "I always ran this car on the street," says Calori. "I didn't have a second car." Calori never had a problem with the fact that he didn't have a starter. The car was so beautiful that it always drew a crowd and there was always somebody who wanted to hear it run. Calori would tell them, "If you'd like to hear it run, start pushing. I never had anyone refuse to push-start it."

The most distinctive components on Calori's A V-8 roadster were the chrome pipes that swept around the

Jack Calori sold his beautiful Model A roadster to Bill Potts, his dentist. Potts put whitewall tires on the front, which Calori hated, and removed the grille insert. Calori drove the car for Potts at El Mirage and blew the transmission. After that, Calori saw the car only once.

sides of the car. When Calori first built his A V-8 roadster, he had the traditional Flathead three-into-one headers that ran below the car. The headers had caps and pipes that ran into mufflers. Ford Flathead V-8 engines had three exhaust ports on each side; the two cylinders in the center of each bank had to share a single port. Calori wanted to insert a baffle in the center port. He then paired up the two front and two rear ports on each side of the engine. Clark Muffler Shop in Compton built the pipes. Even though the pipes were chrome plated, they never discolored or turned blue. Because of the sleek style of the new pipes, there wasn't any room for mufflers. "There were no baffles," says Calori. "Except back then, we had a nice thing known as 'Chore Girl.'" This was a loosely woven, coarse steel wool used for cleaning pots and pans. Calori would force a ball of it down each pipe when not at the lakes. Calori admits that the roadster may have been faster with a shorter set of headers, but he also wanted his car to be distinct. "I wanted it look good too," says Calori. "The fact is, that if the pipes were shorter, it could have been more efficient."

Because of the long headers, the doors on Calori's roadster couldn't be opened. His solution was to weld them shut. Body man Herb Renau smoothed the sides, built the blisters on the hood, and frenched the license plate into the 1932 grille shell. "Herb Renau was the greatest body man there ever was," proclaims Calori. "He could take anything and weld it and there was never a wrinkle. He was a great guy!" Renau also built Calori's custom 1936 Ford coupe that was on the cover of *Hot Rod* magazine.

Spanish red leather covered the interior of Calori's Model A V-8 roadster, with a matching tonneau cover. "The gauges were exploded across the dash," says Calori "In other words, instead of being in a cluster, they went clear across the dash." Calori also had a pump that pressurized a 20 gallon Cadillac gas tank.

When Calori first built his A V-8 roadster, he had brakes on all four wheels. When he installed the hot Flathead, he removed the set on the front. "I took off the front brakes and still drove it on the street," says Calori. "It's like riding a motorcycle, you become adapted to the stopping power."

Calori had one of the most consistent roadsters at the lakes. His procedure was to warm the engine in the morning. "I'd warm it up and get all the lubricants heated. I never changed the spark plugs. I never changed the jets. I didn't do anything but drive it up there and run it, and I never came out less than 3rd fastest." Records show that in SCTA competition, Calori finished the 1946 season in 12th place and in 1947, he placed 3rd. His roadster consistently ran between 124 and 128 miles per hour, and all of his runs were on gasoline.

Calori sold his roadster to his dentist, Bill Potts. Before he delivered it, he took out his engine and swapped in Potts' engine. "He had an engine and transmission which was a 3/8 by 3/8 with Edelbrock manifold and heads," says Calori. "I put it in and got it running. He wanted it timed at El Mirage and I drove it for the first time [for Potts]. The transmission must have been bad because I didn't jam the gears. I put it in second, hit it, and all the gears blew out. That was the end of that."

By the late 1940s, there was an abundance of speed equipment available for the Ford Flathead. This 1932 roadster's later-model Flathead engine is equipped with Edelbrock aluminum heads, a three carburetor intake manifold, and chrome headers. The average hot rodder in the 1940s had the ability to add bolt-on performance components, but usually lacked the sophistication necessary for extensive internal work.

This clean 1927 Model T roadster is V-8 powered and has a set of lengthy chrome exhaust pipes. Long exhaust collectors are not extremely efficient, but they make a distinctive sound. Other features of this red roadster include a 1932 grille shell and a custom hood. Some cardboard has been taped on to streamline the front. The Firestone rear tires were previously used on an Indianapolis race car.

Calori only saw the car one time later, parked at a curb, and he thought it looked a little shabby. It was a sad ending for one of the most beautiful roadsters to ever run on the lakes.

Stu Hilborn's A V-8
Stu Hilborn ran a roadster at the lakes before he built his famous streamliner. After a few trips to the lakes

with his friends, he decided to build a roadster. "I bought the car [Model A roadster] from a used car dealer," says Hilborn. "It was sitting on the lot without an engine. He was having a hard time selling it, but it was just what I wanted." Hilborn was glad it didn't have an engine because he wanted to run a V-8. "I had so much to learn," says Hilborn. "It was nice to start with a roadster because I didn't know anything about tools. I didn't know anything about machinery or engines. It was a learning experience for me." Hilborn's mentor was Eddie Miller. Miller was a former race car driver from Indianapolis with a remarkable set of mechanical skills. "He was the opposite of me—he could do anything," admits Hilborn. "He was a good driver, an excellent engine man, and he could weld sheet metal.

The team of Reiff and Wells, members of the *Idlers* club, entered this B-class roadster at the SCTA meets at El Mirage in 1948. Their car is a channeled 1932 Ford roadster that runs a 1946 Mercury engine with Sharp heads and intake. The car was channeled to lessen the drag. The door hinges and handles were removed, and the doors were welded shut. The custom hood is slightly longer than a stock 1932 hood, and the entire car is painted in black primer. Because of the placement of the front spring, it appears that this roadster has parallel leaves in the front.

I had never done any of those things, or even seen them being done. It turned out to be a godsend for me to learn from someone who had all those skills."

Miller took an interest in Hilborn and his roadster project. He built the engine and ground the cam. "He ground the cam himself, but he didn't have a cam grinder," says Hilborn. Miller made a fixture to hold the cam on-center in front of a regular bench grinder. The fixture allowed forward movement, but didn't provide contour for the cam's lobes. "He'd get the thing roughed in on that fixture. He put bluing all the way around it and then he'd rotate it by hand so far, and

come back and look at it, and then do a little bit more. Then he'd take it over and put an indicator on it to see where he was, and just slowly, day after day, he'd work that through 'til he finally got the lobe where it looked right." At that point, Miller slid the cam in the engine and checked the cam with a dial indicator on top of a valve. This process was exceptionally tedious, but it produced an excellent cam. "That's the only cam I ever used, and it ran great," boasts Hilborn.

Hilborn's roadster was designed to only run on the lakes. He ran it in 1940 and 1941. Eddie Miller's engine was quite powerful and revved higher than

Roadsters were popular at the lakes, and the most popular one of all was the 1932 Ford. It had the most refined lines of any Roadster and came standard with a V-8 or stout four-cylinder engine. A later upgrade to a Flathead was simple. Here, two 1932s are waiting to make their runs down the lake.

Jim Nelson's Wild Roadster Ride

Jim Nelson, a member of the *Oilers* club, ran a channeled 1927 T roadster at the lakes. He installed a military surplus aircraft yolk for the steering wheel. "The wheel was a 3/4 thing with ears sticking up, and this car was so low that when I sat in it, my knees were way up high," says Nelson. One day he was driving the Roadster and went around a big turn. When the wheel came back, the ear on top got caught in the cuff of his pants.

"The roadster continued to turn right, going around a corner, through a ditch until it was launched up, over, and through a barbed wire fence," says Nelson. "The car broke the top and bottom strands of wire because they were rusty, but there was a brand-new piece in the middle—that's the one that caught me under the chin." Nelson didn't have a seatbelt, so the barbed wire jerked him out of the car and flung him onto the rear deck. "I didn't even know what happened. I could see one of the car's wheels turning, and I wanted to shut off the engine," he says. Nelson had taken two wires from the ignition and twisted them together to start and shut off the engine.

When he leaned forward to shut the car off, everything was covered in blood. Nelson recalls, "I just about fainted!"

The group of friends who were in a car that had followed Nelson ran up to see if he survived the accident. "I saw their eyes get as big as saucers," exclaims Nelson. "I'm sure they thought, 'This guy's dead—he's cut his head off.'" The woman who owned the property where the accident happened saw the ruckus in her field and came down to see what was going on. The guy who owned the car that was following Nelson had run out of gas, and he wanted to get Nelson to the hospital as quickly as possible, so he commandeered the lady's car. "We stopped by one doctor on the way to the hospital. He came and looked at me and didn't want anything to do with me. It [the barbed wire] just missed my jugular vein."

Nelson lived to tell the story and went on to build more hot rods and race on the dry lakes. He eventually turned to drag racing, building and racing dragsters that he and partner Dode Martin had built as the Dragmaster team.

most Flathead V-8s. Hilborn installed an Auburn instrument panel. "Almost all the Roadsters tried to get the Auburn dash," says Hilborn. The Auburn instrument panels were very popular because Auburns were the only production cars with a 120-mile-per-hour speedometer. "I was most interested in the tachometer," says Hilborn. "That was the only way I had of knowing how good the engine was running until I got an official timing tag." A tach was the only indication of how the car ran during the test runs on Friday because the timing traps weren't installed. "The way I knew if I gained speed was if the tach came up a little higher." On a Friday test run before a meet, Hilborn's tach registered 5,000 rpm. This was an exceptional feat for a 1940s-era Flathead, and word spread quickly. "Vic Edelbrock found out about it. He was the number *one* man," says Hilborn. He came over to Hilborn and said, "I hear you hit 5,000." Hilborn responded that he, in fact, did hit 5,000 rpm. "Will you take me out and show me?" With that, Hilborn invited Edelbrock into his roadster and they took it out across the lake. When they returned, Edelbrock said, "Yeah, you did. Thank you very much," and went on his way.

Describing those early runs on the lakes, Hilborn says, "The feeling is something I had never felt before. That was my first experience with the feeling of speed. The noise seemed to be louder than I expected. It was very nice. I finally got up into the low 120s, which

Arvel Youngblood, a member of the *Idlers* club, sits in his beautiful, black 1932 Ford roadster and waits for his turn to run. He's wearing a Navy flight jacket, a cloth flying helmet, and goggles. Youngblood's roadster features solid hood sides, which was a slick modification to hot rods in the 1940s.

This deuce roadster features 11 Stewart Warner gauges spread across the width of the instrument panel. One can't help but wonder whether the influence of the World War II military aircraft instrument-filled cockpit was the model for this installation. The owner has installed a banjo steering wheel with a custom hub and column shift.

wasn't too bad a speed for those days, but it wasn't up there with the number one guys, but it was a start." Hilborn eventually became one of the "number one guys" after his sleek, black streamliner set a 150-mile-per-hour record.

Fred Lobello's 1932 Roadster

Fred Lobello of San Diego bought his first roadster in July 1941. It was a black full fendered 1932 Model B. "I went to work in an aircraft plant, and after two weeks, I had earned enough money to buy a car," says Lobello. "I looked in the paper and saw an ad for a 1932 roadster. My dad took me to the address where the roadster was sitting in the driveway." The owner told Lobello he needed to buy some welding equipment and it was going to cost him $65, and that would be the price of the roadster. "I paid the man $65 and drove it home. The only thing that wasn't stock were the two horns under the hood."

This 1932 Ford roadster has been channeled approximately 7 inches. It has a custom hood with plenty of louvers. The chrome exhaust headers extend out from the hood and end just short of the door. The black interior trim has been rolled up and over the top edge of the doors and rear passenger compartment opening.

Fred Lobello (foreground, left) originally bought this 1932 roadster in July of 1941 for $65. He transformed it into a highboy in 1942 and raced it on the lakes between 1945 and 1948. It was powered by the original Model B four-cylinder that received additional modifications each year it was run. By 1948, Lobello consistently ran his street-driven roadster at speeds over 90 mph. In 1949, Lobello pulled the engine and installed it in his new belly tank.

Lobello soon met members of the *San Diego Roadster* club, visited the dry lakes, and turned his roadster into a highboy. Lobello stuck with the four-cylinder engine. "I grew up with them [four-cylinder engines] because my dad had Model A trucks," says Lobello. "I loved the sound of the four-cylinder, it had a different roar than the V-8. The V-8s were a little faster, but some of the four-bangers would go pretty quick too." Lobello drove his deuce roadster on the street and ran it at the lakes between 1945 and 1948. "In 1947, I had the engine running real well," says Lobello. "I had a Smith cam with a Winfield head, two carbs, and a pressurized fueling system. I was trying to pull some 3.27 gears,

but they were too tall." In 1948, Lobello borrowed a Cragar head from a friend. "I drove it on the street and ran it twice at El Mirage, both times I ran over 100 miles per hour." A four-cylinder-powered 1932 that could reach 100 miles per hour was quite an accomplishment in the late 1940s.

When Lobello wasn't racing his deuce roadster, he drove it on the street. "I had a top for it, little sealed beam headlights, and twin 1939 taillights," says Lobello. The roadster also had a split manifold and dual exhaust that exited through the rear of the body. "I removed the seat riser so I could lower the seat, then the gearshift lever became too tall to do any good

Left: Robert Joehnck of the *Whistlers* club ran 119.52 mph in this clean 1929 Ford in the B Roadster class. The frame is from a 1932 Ford, and the engine is a 239-ci Flathead. Hydraulic brakes have been added, along with a dropped front axle with chrome tubular shocks on custom mounts. Joehnck added a custom hood and 1932 grille shell that has been filled. At speeds over 90 mph, this grille's vertical bars produced a distinct whistle.

Below: This B-class roadster belonged to Harvey Haller. It is fitted with a 1929 Model A roadster body that is channeled over a Model T frame. A belly pan has been added, along with a rounded nosepiece for streamlining. The engine is a 1938 Ford 239-ci Flathead with Evans heads and intake manifold. Twin chrome-plated exhaust pipes sweep up each side of the car. A military surplus aluminum bucket seat is barely visible though the tarp that covers the passenger compartment. This Roadster consistently ran between 120 and 128 mph. One of the many food vendor stands is visible in the background.

shifting," says Lobello. "I cut it off to make it shorter, but it still didn't feel right." Lobello told his welder about the uncomfortable feeling of the shifter. "He said, 'Get in the car and put it in low gear.'" The welder pulled out his torch and heated the bottom of the shifter until it was cherry red and told Lobello, "Pull it toward you where it feels the best." The new, shorter arm and repositioning allowed Lobello to speed-shift. Because of the basic design of the clutch, it was much easier to speed-shift a four-cylinder Ford than a V-8. A

It's difficult to understand why the owner of this 1932 roadster welded the doors shut and cut the circular openings in the side of the body. It does feature a nicely outfitted Flathead engine and a unique frame cover that extends from the front spreader bar to the grille. The tall headlight mounts are also an interesting feature.

Opposite, top: The team of Bob Giovanine and Chuck Spurgin ran one of the fastest roadsters on the lakes, and it wasn't a Ford! Before the war, Spurgin bought a 1925 Chevrolet roadster for $25, and Giovanine built a powerful 1925 Chevy four-cylinder engine. After the war, they combined the body with the engine and assaulted the lakes. In 1947, they ran in the B Roadster class and placed 15th in SCTA points. This meant they were allowed to paint the number 15 on the side of their car for the 1948 season. In 1948, they destroked their Chevy engine to allow them into the A Roadster class where they quickly set the record at 123.05 mph for a two-way average. The small pipe sticking out of the rear deck is the exhaust pipe that ran through the inside of the body.

Opposite, bottom: This Model T roadster was run by Paul Schiefer of the *San Diego Roadster* club. Schiefer's car featured a tube chassis and a 1925 Model T body. The engine was a 286-ci 1947 Mercury Flathead with an Edelbrock intake and heads. With Butch Ludwig behind the wheel, it ran the fastest time of any roadster at 148.02 mph at SCTA's July 1948 meet.

Below: The number 1R on the side of Doug Hartelt's roadster indicates it received the most points of any roadster in the previous year's (1947) SCTA competition. Hartelt's Model T roadster was powered by a 1946 Mercury Flathead with Evans heads and intake manifold. It ran in the mid-130-mph range in the B Roadster class. Hartelt was a member of the *Lancers* club.

Owners of Cadillac LaSalle V-8-powered roadsters faced the problem of exhaust ports that exited from the top of the engine. This competitor built an elegant set of upswept chrome-plated headers and a custom hood with openings that matched the pipes. Twin Stromberg carburetors with chrome stacks extend through the center of the hood.

V-8 clutch had three centrifugal weights on the clutch. When the engine rpm went up, the clutch became tighter and more difficult to disengage quickly. "When I was going to shift from low to second, I didn't think about shifting," says Lobello. "All I did was put a little pressure on that lever and pop the clutch and it would be in second gear real quick!"

Lobello put his speed-shifting technique to a test on the streets of San Diego. "One Saturday morning I was going to go to my welding shop," says Lobello. "I made a right turn out of the alley and another guy came down the hill to my left and honked the horn at me. We both stopped at the stop sign and looked at each other and I knew what was going to happen. The next thing I knew, I went across the intersection in low gear, smoking the tires. When I popped the clutch for second gear, the car jumped up and we were side by side. At the end of the block, the road split." Both cars went their separate ways and neither knew what the other had under the hood. "We didn't think we were really street-racing, but I guess it was," says Lobello.

Left: The interior of this roadster (pictured below) has the same high level of detail as the rest of the car. The large steering wheel is from a Lincoln. It also features a column shift, machine-turned instrument cluster, and a radio on the right side of the instrument panel.

Below: This 1932 roadster was one of the nicer examples of a street-driven Roadster that ran at the lakes. It's channeled and is equipped with rare postwar whitewall tires. The Flathead engine is equipped with Offenhauser heads and plenty of chrome trim. The most outstanding features are the chromed headers. They swoop smoothly over the frame rails and blend nicely into the long collector.

Above: I'd be smiling too if I owned this clean 1932 roadster! The attachment on the rear of the frame is an indicator that this roadster was most likely used as a tow car. This roadster features 1939 Ford teardrop taillights, 1940 Ford Standard hubcaps with trim rings, and a finely stitched top with mail-slot rear window.

Opposite, top: Although the exterior workmanship was not outstanding on Harold Daigh's C-class roadster, it was a fast car. The body on Daigh's roadster was a 1927 Ford Model T channeled over Model A rails. The hood and nosepiece were homemade and fit tightly around the 268-ci Mercury engine. Large discs, instead of front brakes, are used to smooth out airflow around the tires. Daigh was a member of the *Dolphins* club and held the SCTA C Roadster record of 140.995 mph in 1948 with this car.

Opposite, bottom: Two of the most favored roadsters were the 1928 and 1929 Fords. They had a small, sleek body with a flared character line at the base of the cowl. This roadster features front and rear split radius rods. The standard dry lakes tire combination of small diameter on the front and large diameter on the rear is quite apparent on this roadster.

A 1928 or 1929 Model A roadster with a V-8 engine was called an "A V-8." This A V-8 was run by Bill Braun of the *Gear Grinders* club. It features Kelsey-Hayes wire wheels, split radius rods, a custom hood, and a 1932 grille shell. The interior appears to be fully trimmed in green vinyl or leather. Powered by a 1941 Ford Flathead, the roadster ran 122.95 mph at El Mirage. A Fisk tire truck can be seen in the background.

Tommy Tompkins' blue 1932 roadster was one of the most contemporary hot rods in 1948. It featured a hood with solid sides and solid disc wheels with hubcaps and trim rings. This style hood was stylish, but created a cooling problem for Flathead engines that often overheated. The solid disc wheels were replacements for the Kelsey-Hayes wire wheels that most hot rodders used in the late 1930s and early 1940s. Tompkins' roadster was powered by a 1941 Mercury engine with Offenhauser equipment, and the roadster reached 115.83 mph at El Mirage. Tompkins was a member of the *Sidewinders*.

Keith Landrigan's Channeled 1932 roadster

Not all roadsters that ran at the lakes were powered by Ford Flatheads or by four-cylinder engines. Keith Landrigan's channeled 1932 Ford ran a 1938 Cadillac LaSalle Flathead V-8. The engine looks similar to a Ford Flathead, except the exhaust ports exit from the top of the block. Landrigan's roadster was so finely detailed that it was selected as the cover car for the second issue of *Hot Rod* magazine.

Before the war, Landrigan ran several Model Ts at the lakes and was a member of the *Flyers* club. During the war, he served as an Aviation Machinist Mate on the carriers *Essex*, *Lexington*, and *Yorktown*. He tuned the engines on Navy Corsairs and Hellcat fighters for

For easy entry and exit, the leather interior of Landrigan's Roadster is rolled over the top of the passenger compartment opening. A small chrome-plated gauge panel is mounted at the base of the steering column. To the right of that panel is the white knob of the hand pump that provides pressure to the fuel tank. Both the steering wheel and column shift are from a 1940 Ford. A pair of Stromberg carburetors sticks through the hood.

some of the most important battles of the Pacific. After the war, Landrigan built his uniquely powered roadster. The engine was a 1938 Lasalle that was ported and relieved. It was bored .155 inch, and a full-race Winfield cam was added. The Arco heads were milled .040 inch, and special exhaust valves were installed. Landrigan's Roadster ran 115.83 miles per hour at El Mirage.

One of the most distinctive features of Landrigan's roadster was the long headers that emerged out of the hood and swept back along the side of the body. Small mufflers were hidden in the long collector pipes. The length of the pipes and their proximity to the side of the car restricted the roadster's doors from opening. This was not a problem because many of the street roadsters in the 1940s had doors that were welded

shut. For easy entry, the interior padding was wrapped up and over the edge of the passenger compartment. Landrigan's roadster had a 1940 Ford steering wheel with a column shift and a small panel with Stewart Warner gauges.

Roadsters were the cornerstones of the early dry lakes racers. They were seen as true hot rods, unlike coupes and sedans, which were viewed as family transportation cars. Roadsters were also the entry-level cars for most enthusiasts. They were inexpensive, and most modifications could be made with simple tools. Parts, and even entire cars, could be found at a local wrecking yard. The classic look—highboy, dropped front axle, big-'n' little tires—was established by the early hot rod pioneers, and this style still looks good today.

Opposite: Keith Landrigan's navy blue 1932 roadster was on the cover of the second issue of *Hot Rod* magazine in February 1948. It has been channeled and is powered by a 1938 LaSalle engine. The upswept exhaust headers facilitate the engine's exhaust ports that exit out of the top of the engine. The long collector where the mufflers are located requires the doors to be welded shut. Landrigan's D-class roadster ran 115.83 mph on El Mirage. A temporary hood was added to comply with SCTA rules. The ice cream truck in the background is typical of the food vendors who came out to sell to the hot and hungry crowd.

123

COUPES, MODIFIED ROADSTERS, BELLY TANKS, & STREAMLINERS

Belly tanks were one of the most unique race cars designed to run on the dry lakes. The tanks were initially designed as auxiliary fuel tanks for World War II fighters, but their aerodynamic teardrop shape and size were perfect for the dry lakes. This is one of the larger 315-gallon tanks designed for a P-38. It was 36 inches in diameter—just big enough to tuck a Flathead engine in the rear. This belly tank was raced by Burke and Francisco, driven by Wally Parks, and it has the number 1 on its side, which means it was the SCTA high-points champion for the previous year.

The quest for speed took many forms at the dry lakes. Roadsters were the mainstay, but many competitors built other types of cars. With the exception of stock-bodied roadsters, the classification of the other cars that ran at the lakes constantly changed. The Modified class consisted of basic roadsters that had been modified. This included a narrowed roadster (or custom) body that was designed for competition only. Early streamliners were modified with an added tail section. After the war, a new breed of streamliners evolved from the World War II belly tank. These belly tanks were bought as surplus items and were easily converted into race cars.

The coupe body style was the odd man out in the SCTA. It was regarded as family transportation and not a true hot rod. Drivers who wanted to run their coupes on the lakes formed the Russetta Timing Association.

The term lakester was introduced in the late 1940s when the SCTA determined that smaller Model T roadsters had an unfair advantage over the larger 1932 models and placed the roadsters in a class of their own. The Lakester class eventually included belly tanks; and cars with sleek bodies and covered tires were placed in the

When the SCTA was first formed, there were three classes for lakes cars: Roadsters, Streamliners, and Modifieds. Modifieds and streamliners were very similar except the modified didn't have a rear body. By the late 1940s, all modifieds ran in the Streamliner class. This is Phil Remington's modified/streamliner as it looked in 1948. Remington was a member of the *Low Flyers* club. On June 6, 1948, he drove this car to a speed of 128.75 mph.

George Olalson, a member of the *Pasadena Roadster club*, drove this Modified to a speed of 116.27 mph at El Mirage in April 1948. It was powered by a 1941 Ford Flathead with stock heads and a Navarro intake. The Model T body has been narrowed and painted with flames, and it has a 1932 grille shell.

Streamliner class. The classification of lakes cars continually evolved as the sport matured, and as racers found new and interesting cars to build and race.

Modifieds

The Modified class consisted of severely cut-down roadsters. Modifieds featured bodies that were hacked, chopped, narrowed, and channeled. While most were built from Ford bodies, almost any body make would do as a starting point. The rear deck portion, often called a turtle deck, was left off and a small gas tank was added above the rear axle. Racers added grille shells that were more narrow, sleek, and smooth than the original pieces. The grilles were either a narrow

This unidentified driver looks rather confident perched on top of the seat back of his modified. The car is powered by a Flathead V-8 and has a set of exhaust stacks made from flex tubing. The small cylinder on the side of the cowl is a pump that provides air pressure to the fuel tank. One of the most unusual features of this car is the roll bar, which helps identify the car's history. The car was originally run in the 1930s by Orville "Snuffy" Welchel. It went through a series of owners, engines, and other modifications, and finally ended up with Art and Lloyd Chrisman. They lengthened the wheelbase and took it to the drag strip. With Art at the wheel, it was the first car to break the 9-second barrier. It was also the ribbon cutter at the NHRA's First National Championship drag races at Great Bend, Kansas, in 1955.

production version, or a custom-made nose. Hoods were a class requirement, and most were handmade. Race car center-steering units were installed because of the narrow, single-seat bodies. Chassis were built from any straight frame rails, and most of the frame rails and running gear were from various Ford products.

A wide variety of highly modified Ford four-cylinder engines fit neatly under the narrow hoods of the early modifieds. As the Flathead V-8s became pop-

Modifieds represented the bridge between stock roadsters and streamliners. The body on this one appears to be custom made with the exception of the grille shell. The rear wheels are the seldom-used Ford wire wheels. Most competitors used the stronger Kelsey-Hayes wire wheels. While waiting in line to race, the young man in this photo offered the young lady the more comfortable seat behind the wheel.

Clem Tebow's modified was built from a 1926 Model T body. It ran a 1946 Mercury engine that displaced 272 cubic inches and was equipped with Weiand heads and intake manifold. Tebow's modified was one of the more attractive cars on the lakes in 1949, but it ran far off the class record at 115.83 mph.

Early modifieds were often hastily assembled like this Flathead-powered Model T. With the exception of a dual-intake manifold, the engine appears to be stock right down to the exhaust manifolds. The man hustling through the center of the frame, wearing the leather flight jacket with a camera around his neck, is Don Cox.

One of the trademark features of a modified is a very narrow body. Most bodies consisted of early roadster shells with a large section removed from the center. A sprint car style center steering gear was added. Many modifieds initially used four-cylinder engines that fit neatly under the narrow hood. As V-8s became more popular, they were installed in the older modifieds and extended beyond the confines of the hood.

In 1948, the team of Path and Moore of the *Lancers* club ran this car, a former modified, in the B Streamliner class. The frame was from an early Chevy, and the body was custom-built. It was powered by a 1948 Mercury engine and ran a respectable 133.13 mph at the SCTA meet at El Mirage in August 1948.

In 1949, the team of Path and Moore returned to the dry lakes. They raced the same car that they had run in 1948, with the exception of an added tail section. The 16-inch wire wheels on this car were manufactured by Kelsey-Hayes and were stronger than the ones produced by Ford.

ular due to the availability of speed equipment, many of the modifieds were retrofitted with the V-8. Because modifieds were not intended for street use, although a few may have been street-driven, the engine's exhaust headers joined into a large pipe that ran down the side of the car, similar to a midget race car. Early modifieds easily ran speeds of 100 to 110 miles per hour, thanks to the small frontal area, lightweight, and a moderately hopped-up four-cylinder engine. The modifieds eventually folded into the Lakester class in the late 1940s.

Streamliners

The Streamliner class initially developed from the Modified class. The only difference between the two was an added tail section to the streamliner. Eventually, custom-built race cars were added to the class. streamliners were classified as roadsters according to the engine's cubic-inch displacement. The first streamliners lacked sophisticated aerodynamic techniques, but instinct drove the early racers to make modifications. Their seat-of-the-pants aerodynamic work was done without the aid of computers or wind tunnels.

The most famous streamliner to run the lakes was Stu Hilborn's slick, black machine. It was originally built and run at the lakes by Bill Warth. At the end of the 1941 season, Warth decided to quit racing and sell the car. "I heard about the car being for sale and went down to look at it," says Hilborn. "He wanted to know what I was going to do with it, and I told him I was going to put a V-8 in it and run at the lakes." Warth had run a four-cylinder engine in the car and didn't think a V-8 would fit. "I thought it would, so I told him I'd like to buy the car." Hilborn paid $75 for the car without an engine or transmission and told Warth that

The easiest way to fit into the Streamliner class at the lakes in the 1940s was to buy a race car with a tail section. Like many of the streamliners, this one obviously also ran on the circle tracks as a sprint car. It's powered by a four-cylinder engine with an exquisite header pipe.

133

Bob Weinberg, a member of the *Gaters* club, showed up at the September 1948 meet at El Mirage with this slick, hand-built roadster. It was placed in the D Streamliner class because of its supercharged 1946 Mercury engine and custom body. Gus Maanum's drawing of this car was featured on the cover of the October 1948 SCTA racing program.

Quarter Milers club members Henrich and Seaton raced this unusually styled C streamliner at an SCTA meet in 1948, where it ran 112.07 mph. Ralph Schenck built this streamliner in 1940. Schenck's best speed was 126.89 mph with a Chevy four-cylinder engine.

he'd be back the following Sunday to pick up the car. "I came back the following Sunday to pick it up. As we were loading it on the trailer, his wife came out of the house and said that Pearl Harbor had just been bombed." Hilborn stored the car at his house for the duration of the war while he was in the service.

Hilborn completed his streamliner after the end of World War II. The sleek body was all steel and beautifully constructed. "It was all hand-formed out of sheet steel, not aluminum. When I wrecked that thing, it was wrinkled up just like a ball of twisted metal. Eddie Miller hammered the whole thing out and straightened it." The chassis had a combination of Ford and Chevrolet components. The front axle from a 1937 Ford was streamlined with the addition of wood and canvas. The rear end, with 3.27 gears, was from a

Model A with reversed 1932 housings. The first time Hilborn drove the car on the lakes, there was a significant amount of vibration through the chassis. "Most streamliners didn't have springs," says Hilborn. "The lakebed was usually smooth enough that they weren't necessary. There was a considerable amount of vibration because it had no springs, but we eventually put springs on the streamliner." The streamliner's large-diameter wheels were covered, inside and out, with large discs to smooth the airflow over the tires. The cramped cockpit had a butterfly-style aircraft steering wheel. "I just had rear brakes," recalls Hilborn. "You really never needed a brake [at the lakes] because once you ran through the traps, you'd just get off the throttle and it would slow down by itself."

Stu Hilborn's streamliner was the first lakes car to run 150 mph. It was originally built and raced by Bill Warth. When Hilborn bought it, he installed the V-8 60 he ran his roadster. Much of the development work Hilborn (pictured at rear of the car in white T-shirt and goggles) did on his first fuel-injection system was done on this car.

Hilborn, like most lakes competitors, was limited by the rear-end gear ratio of 3.27. "I had the problem of trying to get enough gear ratio," says Hilborn. "I bought the highest rear-end gear that was available." In an attempt to solve the gearing problem, he built his own overdrive transmission. "I started out with a full transmission with three speeds, but there was still too much power. What I did was eliminate reverse and build a little gear arrangement inside the transmission that provided overdrive. I started off in high gear and I'd shift into overdrive. That brought my gear ratio much closer, but I was still too low."

Once the SCTA decided to race at Bonneville, a place where higher speeds could be attained, Alex Xydias built a streamliner. "In the winter of 1948 is when we found out [we] were going to go to Bonneville," says Xydias. "That was going to be exciting. I thought, let's do something special if we're going to go to Bonneville." His unorthodox approach and switch to a streamliner brought a lot of criticism. Dean Batchelor showed Xydias a book on Auto Union. "It had all the wind tunnel tests on their streamliners. The bottom line of these tests was that they enclosed one

Above: Stu Hilborn had to turn sideways to squeeze into the driver's seat of his streamliner. Hilborn is dressed like the typical 1940s-era lakes driver with a cloth flight helmet, goggles, and leather jacket.

Right: Marvin Lee was the owner of this B streamliner. The engine was a 1947 Chevy six-cylinder engine that displaced 247 cubic inches. It was modified with a Wayne head and intake manifold. On July 17, 1949, it ran a one-way speed of 160.42 mph and set a new two-way record of 153.545 mph.

of the Grand Prix cars in a streamlined body that increased the frontal area by 50 percent, but they reduced the drag by 50 percent." Batchelor came up with a design that was somewhat similar to that of a streamliner run by the Spalding brothers in 1939. That car was not spectacular, and many people predicted the same for Xydias.

Neil Emory at Valley Custom built the streamliner body on his existing belly tank chassis. "Every night we would go out there," says Xydias. "Dean, Keith Baldwin, other friends, and I would do all the grunt work, like riveting the side panels—anything that was flat. Neil [Emory] would do all the hard work on the

aluminum." The naysayers felt the car was too big. "When we took it to the lakes for the first time to test it, the wheel wells weren't covered and it was in bare aluminum. It really did look like we were going the wrong way." After a few shakedown runs on El Mirage, Xydias headed for Bonneville.

Before the war, the fastest hot rods ran 140 miles per hour. After the war, speeds jumped to 150, then 155. The speeds inched up 1 or 2 miles per hour at a time when Xydias hoped he could change that trend. Xydias and Batchelor knew that because of the altitude of Bonneville, they would lose a little horsepower. The loss of horsepower would be more than

Alex Xydias and Dean Batchelor teamed up to design and build a streamliner for the 1949 SCTA season, and hoped to race it at Bonneville. Batchelor designed the car and Neil Emory built it at Valley Custom. Most competitors thought the car was too big and had an inefficient aerodynamic design. This streamliner was the fastest car at Bonneville in 1949 and 1950. The car ran at speeds up to 250 mph. The taped-over damage on the nose of the So-Cal Streamliner occurred when the left rear fender of Batchelor's 1939 Ford coupe touched it in a towing mishap.

compensated for by the high quality of the salt surface. Expectations were high for record speeds in all classes, so timer Otto Crocker made up a new timing chart that listed speeds up to 175 miles per hour. A few weeks prior to Bonneville, at El Mirage, Bill Burke's belly tank clicked off a speed of 160 miles per hour, and added more speculation to record speeds. Batchelor's first run in the So-Cal Streamliner was a mild 150 miles per hour. "Our first run was a tune-up run," says Xydias. "We ran 170 and certainly was going 200. All the naysayers felt that they had accurately predicted the car's failure. Batchelor didn't hold back on the next run. It looked fast and every-

one waited around the timing tower to hear the speed. After a long wait someone asked the timing crew, "How fast did he go?" The response was, "It went off the chart!" Crocker's new speed chart was now obsolete. "We made this quantum leap," marveled Xydias. "It went 187 and then 193 on the record run." In doing so, Batchelor lost the rubber off of his Firestone tires. "They were only guaranteed to 175, but nobody had ever worried about that before," says Xydias. "They tore up the whole tires real bad, but the carcass didn't blow. At Bonneville in 1950, Batchelor stepped up the speed to 210 miles per hour. "We upped the hot rod record 50 miles per

The Cost of Hot Rodding in the 1940s

In 1940, the average factory worker made approximately $20 a week, and a gas station attendant made $10. By today's standards, these paychecks seem miniscule, but at that time, the cost of living was a lot lower. The cost of a hot rod was downright reasonable.

Here's an ad Fred Dunn of Fullerton, California, placed in the March 1940 edition of the *SCTA's Racing News*: Buick four in '30 A, V-8 wheels, good rubber, new V-8 front axle, new 3.27 gears, Riley ground cam, 7:1 compression, new brakes, '31 steering, 1940 license plates paid for, cost over $300, full price $75.

By 1947, hot rod prices had risen slightly. In the January 1947, edition of the *California Timing News*, Ladd Westhoven of Compton, California, placed this ad for a hot Flathead engine and confirmed that coupes were seen as family cars and were not very popular in Southern California: Full race motor complete, ready to run including generator, clutch, and pressure plate. '46 Mercury block, '39 Ford crankshaft, 3 5/16 bore, Visel pistons, Bertran Cam, adjustable lifters, Thickston 10:1 heads,

Weiand manifold, 97 carbs, Zepher ignition, Clay Smith 19-lb flywheel, motor run less than 500 miles, timed SCTA Modified 129.49. Price—$475. '32 Ford three-window coupe body—$35, '32 Ford frame—$25.

One year later, the January 1948, *California Timing News* had the following three ads:

Charles Pepper of Los Angeles offered his '32 Roadster for sale: Roadster—Clean '32, 3 5/16 bore Weiand manifold, Offenhauser heads, headers, good paint, upholstery, and top, $900.

Mark Cravens of Los Angeles offered the following four-cylinder-powered Roadster: '29A "B" block, Fargo four-port, hydraulic brakes, V-8 trans, drilled C crank, special rods, ignition, and headers, three different intake manifolds, new tires, Kelsey wheels, $650.

Lee Enfiajian of Los Angeles, had one complete '32 coupe and two other Model T bodies for sale: '32 five-window coupe—$295, '27 T Roadster body—$50, '27 T pickup cab—$15.

The 1940 Mercury engine in Emil Dietrich's streamliner was built by Regg Schlemmer. Schlemmer was a lakes racer who also owned a speed shop and built high-performance engines. This car reached 144.46 mph at the April 1948 SCTA meet at El Mirage.

The text on the car reads: REGG SCHLEMMER SPECIAL MOTOR

hour in two years," says Xydias. "We only wanted to be the fastest hot rod—that's all we wanted, but it was significant because it was the fastest American car ever built!"

Xydias and Batchelor's So-Cal Streamliner recast the mold for the design of future streamliners and higher speeds by American competitors. His accomplishments confirmed what the SCTA told the Salt Lake committee a few years earlier—that hot rods could go fast.

Belly Tanks

Belly tanks, also known as drop tanks or wing tanks, were external fuel tanks that were added to the underside of the fuselage or wing hard points on fighter aircraft. These tanks added enough extra fuel to allow the P-51 Mustangs and P-38 Lightnings to escort B-17 and B-24 bombers to their targets as far away as Germany, and return back to base in England. These tanks were used on the outbound leg of the sortie, and dropped when the tanks were empty. After the war, Los Angeles-area aircraft manufacturers and surplus yards sold these tanks for pennies on the dollar.

Because of the unique design of each World War II fighter, each type of plane had its own specific belly tank. The largest tank was used on the P-38 Lightning. It was designed to carry 315 gallons of fuel, and was 36 inches in diameter. Many of the smaller tanks that were used on P-51 Mustangs and Navy F4U Corsairs were 24 inches in diameter and designed to hold 165 gallons of fuel. These tanks were constructed from aluminum. Because they were expendable, the tanks were made in large quantities as cheaply as possible.

Bill Burke is credited as being the father of the belly tank racer. He went to the lakes for the first time in 1934 and he raced roadsters and modifieds. Like so many of the racers who supported the war effort, Burke joined the Coast Guard during World War II. While he looked at a barge full of belly tanks during his time in the South Pacific, he was inspired to build

In 1947, Emil Dietrich drove this Mercury-powered C-class streamliner in SCTA competition and garnered the most points of any streamliner. This allowed him to run with the number 1 on the side of his car in 1948. This car was previously a modified driven by Ken Lindley and was converted by Dietrich to a "tail job," as streamliners were affectionately known.

Driver Johnny Johnson is in the driver's seat of this Burke & Francisco C-class streamliner. On April 24, 1948, this car set a one-way record of 149.97 mph and a two-way record of 144.86 mph at El Mirage. The frame on this belly tank is from a 1927 Model T, and the 1946 Mercury engine displaced 272 cubic inches.

one of the sleekest and simplest racers of all time. "There was a barge full of wing tanks," says Burke. "I got to looking at them and I thought, 'Holy Toledo— that looks like it would make a wonderful streamliner.' I went over on the barge to measure a tank. Then I was sure that one would be ideal for the dry lakes."

After Burke was discharged in 1946, he drove down Alameda Street in Los Angeles to the junkyards where Southern California hot rodders found old cars and parts. He spotted some surplus belly tanks, bought one, and built his first streamliner. The tank he bought was one of the smaller, 165-gallon models. Because of its size, he put the engine in the front. "It

was so very small I had to crouch in the back behind the motor," says Burke. "It had a solid drive shaft, and I put a bicycle seat on the drive shaft. That's what I sat on." At the same Alameda Street junkyard, Burke also found a larger P-38 tank. "It was bigger and gave me enough room to allow the driver to sit up front and to put the engine in the rear." This mid-engine (engine between the driver and the rear axle) configuration became the standard for belly tank design. Because of its extended teardrop shape, the largest cross section was near the center of the tank. Most of the room was used for the engine, and the driver was cramped in the front. In later years, a few com-

For $60, Bill Burke built a basic chassis for Alex Xydias. Xydias added a Flathead engine, belly tank body and finished the car. He eventually painted the car gold and white with the Su-Cal Speed Shop name on the side. The car is pictured at El Mirage in April 1948, just prior to a shakedown run of 87.04 mph. By the end of the year, it would own the A Streamliner record at 130.355 mph.

Fred Lobello ran a 1932 Roadster for several years at the dry lakes. When he saw how simply belly tank cars were built, he decided to build one for himself and used the four-cylinder engine from his roadster. Lobello's tank, named the *Lady Bug*, was built from the smaller 165-gallon version used on a Navy Corsair. Lobello paid $7 for the tank at a salvage yard, and built a frame out of steel tubing. The rear tires are 700-20 Firestone Deluxe Champion Indianapolis-style tires.

In 1951, Lobello took his belly tank to the Paradise Mesa drag strip in San Diego. He needed a running start because his car, like most belly tanks, was direct-drive with no transmission.

Bill Burke built his very first belly tank in 1946. It was designed with the engine in the front. Burke installed a bicycle seat on the drive shaft to sit as low as possible. This unidentified belly tank was also built with a front engine. Because of the placement of the rear axle and transmission, this configuration forced the driver to be out in the wind stream and negated any aerodynamic advantage of the tank's design.

petitors added several inches of length in the center. Burke raced his own belly tank that was driven by Wally Parks, and he built many belly tank cars for other competitors.

Fred Lobello parked his 1932 roadster and built a belly tank after he saw Bill Burke's car at the lakes. "In 1947, I decided to build a belly tank," says Lobello. "There was a surplus yard in San Diego where you could see the tanks sticking above the fence. I paid $7 for it." The tank that Lobello bought was the smaller 165-gallon version from a Navy Corsair. "Next door was a wrecking yard where I found a 1937 Ford tubular axle that I put on the car." Lobello's parents were not too happy about him racing his Roadster at the lakes, and he knew they would be very unhappy if they knew he was building something that would go even

Ford's small Flathead engine fit snugly in the rear of a belly tank, and the exhaust pipes were ported directly out the side. The throttle linkage was a bit complex, but the lack of a transmission simplified the driveline installation. A handle connected to a cable was used to actuate the clutch. A large water tank was located in front of the engine in place of a radiator. The instrument in front of the driver's compartment is a tachometer.

Don Francisco (wearing sunglasses) leads a discussion at the front of the Burke & Francisco belly tank. The other tall gentleman with his back to the camera, wearing white *Road Runners* overalls, is Wally Parks, the driver of Francisco's belly tank. It was on this day, August 29, 1948, that Parks set the one-way record of 153.32 mph in the C Streamliner class. The tank is equipped with 21-inch Indianapolis tires on the front, and 18-inch Indianapolis tires on the rear. The vehicle used a homemade set of differential gears to increase the ratio for more speed. In the background, another belly tank is being worked on in the shade of a tarp.

Although all belly tanks were designed strictly for lakes racing, this one was designed to be driven on the street. The owner started with a large P-38 tank and added all the equipment necessary, including a side mirror, to drive it on the street. The entire tank was positioned higher on the chassis so the driver had more room. The front of this tank was opened up and a grille was fitted so a radiator could be installed.

faster. His secret project was built at a friend's garage where other friends pitched in to help. The tank was cut in two along the welded side seam. The frame began with two pieces of chrome moly tubing that were curved to fit the inside of the tank. The engine, a

Winfield four, was borrowed from his roadster. "It took us three years to build," says Lobello. "When we were ready to move the car out of the garage, we had to enlarge the garage door to get it out." Lobello's first trip to the dry lakes with his belly tank was in October

1950. "That engine went 96 miles per hour in the Roadster, and 116 in the belly tank," says Lobello. The additional 20 miles per hour was gained strictly through the difference in aerodynamics between the 1932 Roadster and the belly tank.

One of the most famous belly tanks was the So-Cal Speed Shop car. Alex Xydias built the car as an advertisement for his growing speed shop business. "I was So-Cal Speed Shop, not So-Cal Custom Shop," says Xydias. "I knew I had to start to race." Xydias wanted something different to catch every-one's attention. "There were so many roadsters at the lakes, you had to be [Vic] Edelbrock or [Randy] Shinn to catch somebody's eye." Bill Burke built the basic chassis and used a Model T frame. "This was a P-38 tank. They were $15. Cattle ranchers were buying them to use as water troughs for their cattle. They would lay half a tank out in the field and fill it with water." Once Xydias had the car back at his shop, he added water and fuel tanks, and the pedals. Valley Custom built the sleek headrest and painted the car gold and white.

In 1948, Kenny Parks of the *Gaters* club drove this channeled Model T Roadster in the SCTA's C Roadster class where he ran 127.65 mph. In 1949, this car was classified as a lakester. Parks', built by brother Wally, was the first lakes Roadster to feature a belly tank nose. The belly tank pan was an inverted roof from a 1940 Ford Sedan. This was an inexpensive way to add streamlining to an existing car.

The Lodes brothers had Bill Burke build them this belly tank. Here, the rear top half has been removed for access to the V-8 60 Flathead engine. The small round tank in the rear is for fuel, and the larger tank in the front of the engine is for water.

Stu Hilborn sold his streamliner in the early 1950s. It showed up in Edna, Kansas, for an NHRA drag meet in 1954. The streamliner couldn't compete because it did not have a required roll bar, but it was allowed one test run where it reached a speed of 107 mph.

Xydias selected a V-8 60 to power his belly tank. That particular engine was small enough to be lifted in and out of the car by two men. These engines were exceptionally popular with midget racers, and all of the speed equipment available for the larger Flathead was made for the little V-8 60. "I learned to drive without going too fast," says Xydias. "Everything was slower and easier. We had a lot of fun with that V-8 60, in fact, we ran the butt off that thing!" Eventually belly tanks were included in the Streamliner class, and then in the Lakester class.

Lakesters

Lately, the term "Lakester" has often been used to describe any car that ever ran on the lakes. A better definition is a lakes car that is not a stock-bodied roadster. The Lakester class came about in 1949 as the SCTA went to Bonneville. It was used to provide

The Pierson brothers' coupe was one of the most beautiful to ever run on the lakes. Its slanted A-pillars provided a streamlined shape and maintained the minimum windshield height. Coupes were not allowed to run in SCTA sanctioned events until 1950, when the SCTA established a Coupe class. Coupe owners who wanted to run on the lakes joined the Russetta Timing Association (RTA), where they were welcomed.

The deeply slanted A-pillars, track-style nose, and channeled body set the style for the lakes coupe as much as the 1932 highboy did for the lakes Roadster. This coupe has an unusual set of four, widely spaced pipes that stick out from the side of the hood.

a separation between stock-bodied roadsters and modified roadsters. Cars that competed in the Lakester class were initially required to be equipped with an American-made roadster body of a 1927 manufacture or earlier. The body was to be stock in height, width, and contour. Streamlining was allowed in the form of a belly pan or special nose. The mini-

mum wheelbase for a lakester was 95 inches. In 1950, the Lakester class included any car with a body that was 36 inches or less wide, and had open wheels. This now included belly tanks which, due to their shape, were inherently faster than roadsters. Initially, the SCTA allowed any closed car to run in the Lakester class.

Don Cox, this book's photographer, ran roadsters at the lakes until the SCTA allowed coupes. He raced this 1934 five-window at the lakes and drag strips. The roll bar is barely visible through the quarter window. In 1951, Cox ran 112.50 mph with this car in SCTA's B Coupe class.

Coupes

The general feeling among lakes racers was that Roadsters were the only "real" hot rods, and that coupes and sedans were simply family transportation. Coupes and sedans were too big, boxy, and heavy to be serious contenders against a roadster, and the SCTA refused to allow them to compete. This forced those wishing to run at the lakes with a closed car to join an organization that allowed them to compete, such as the Russetta Timing Association, which formed in 1948. Eventually, the SCTA allowed coupes to run in the Lakester class.

The coupes and sedans of the 1920s were boxy and burdened with a large windshield that acted like a speed brake. In a race between a similarly powered 1929 Ford roadster and a 1929 Ford coupe, the roadster would easily win. This mindset became so ingrained that coupes were excluded from events and were always thought of as a poor body for a race car. When Ford released its new V-8 and smoothly styled body in 1932, this bias started to change. The slanted windshields and chopped tops increased the coupe's attractiveness.

The sleek 1934 Ford coupe the Pierson brothers ran changed everyone's attitude toward coupes. It was

heavily chopped with a severely slanted windshield and a race car's styled nose. At the 1950 Bonneville meet, it ran 149.005 miles per hour. Many imitators used Pierson's coupe as a template for their own race car.

The dry lakes have been the home of automotive inventiveness for decades. Cars of all shapes and sizes ran at the lakes and helped open the hot rodders' fertile minds. Early hot rodders transformed a car with a small frontal area and narrowed roadsters into modifieds. With a little added bodywork, these cars were transformed into streamliners. After World War II, belly tanks were very popular because they were unique race cars that were inexpensive and could be built fast. As car styles changed, so did the class structure at the lakes. Inventiveness and creativity have always been encouraged and rewarded in the world of

The interest in coupes skyrocketed once the SCTA allowed coupes to run and drag racing became popular. This 1932 three-window highboy is one of the nicer coupes that drove the streets and raced on the lakes of Southern California in 1951. The dropped front axle and front brake backing plates were chromed. The headlights have an artfully crafted mounting bar, and the front spreader bar has been V'ed and chrome plated.

hot rodding. It was this spirit, along with a great deal of courage, that drove the early hot rodders' achievements. Today, dry lakes racing is seen as one of the purest forms of motor racing. No big sponsors, no television coverage, and no product endorsements. One of the most amazing things is that they still race at El Mirage strictly for the love of speed.

Don Cox has been taking pictures since he was 10 years old. He was a Navy photographer during World War II and served in the Pacific theater. After the war, he visited the dry lakes and became a lifelong hot rodder. Cox raced various cars as a member of the *Oilers* club, and he brought along his cameras and documented the cars, people, and culture of the dry lakes. Here, he sits in one of his favorite roadsters.

BIBLIOGRAPHY

Books

Batchelor, Dean. *The American Hot Rod*. Osceola, WI: MBI Publishing Company, 1995.

Carroll, William. *Muroc: When The Hot Rods Ran*. San Marcos, CA: Auto Book Press, 1991.

Darlington, David. *The Mojave*. New York, NY: Henry Holt and Company Inc., 1996.

Drake, Albert. *Flat Out: California Dry Lake Time Trials 1930-1950*. Portland, OR: Flat Out Press, 1994.

Editors of *Hot Rod* Magazine. *Hot Rods*. Los Angeles, CA: Trend Inc., 1951.

Editors of *Hot Rod* Magazine. *Hot Rod Magazine The First 12 Issues*. Osceola, WI: MBI Publishing Company, 1998.

Hill, George. *1956 Hot-Rod Handbook*. Chicago, IL: Popular Mechanics Company, 1956.

Hop Up Products and Mark Morton. *Hop Up The First 12 Issues*. St. Paul, MN: MBI Publishing Company, 2002.

Montgomery, Don. *Hot Rods in The Forties*. Fallbrook, CA: Don Montgomery, 1987.

Orr, Veda. *Veda Orr's Hot Rod Pictorial*, Los Angeles, CA: Floyd Clymer Publishing, 1949.

Magazines

"Where Are They Now?" *American Rodder*, February 1993.

"What's Behind the SCTA." *Throttle*, January 1941.

"Speed Isn't Everything!" *Hot Rod*, February 1951.

Newsletters and Racing Programs

Associated Club News, July 1938.

California Timing News, January 1947.

California Timing News, March 1947.

California Timing News, April 1947.

California Timing News, January 1948.

First Annual Bonneville National Speed Trials Program, August 1949.

Muroc Dry Lake Amateur Roadster Races, July 1932.

Muroc Dry Lake Amateur Roadster Races, June 1933.

Muroc Dry Lake Time Trials, May 1937.

Roadster Races Muroc Lakes, May 1932.

Russetta Timing Association Official Program, May 1949.

Russetta Timing Association Official Program, July 1949.

Russetta Timing Association Official Program, November 1948.

SCTA Racing News, May 15, 1939.

SCTA Racing News, September 1941.

SCTA Racing News, February 1945.

SCTA Racing News, May 1945.

SCTA Racing News, September 1945.

SCTA Racing News, December 1945.

SCTA Racing News, February 1946.

SCTA Racing News, July 1946.

SCTA Racing News, July 1947.

SCTA Racing News, August 1947.

SCTA Racing News, October 1947.

SCTA Racing News, April 1948.

SCTA Racing News, June 1948.

SCTA Racing News, July 1948.

SCTA Racing News, August 1948.

SCTA Racing News, September 1948.

SCTA Racing News, October 1948.

SCTA Racing News, May 1949.

SCTA Racing News, June 1949.

SCTA Racing News, October 1949.

SCTA Racing News, June 1950.

SCTA Racing News, July 1950.

SCTA Racing News, May 1950.

SCTA Racing News, May 1961.

Southern California Championship Sweepstakes, October 1927.

INDEX